THE GAELIC GARDEN OF THE DEAD

Mac Gillebhrath

Garadh Gaidlig nam Marbh

MACGILLIVRAY

THE GAELIC GARDEN OF THE DEAD

BLOODAXE BOOKS

ISBN: 978 1 78037 443 7

First published 2019 by
Bloodaxe Books Ltd
Eastburn
South Park
Hexham
Northumberland NE46 1BS

www.bloodaxebooks.com
For further information about Bloodaxe titles
please visit our website or write to
the above address for a catalogue.

Supported using public funding by
**ARTS COUNCIL
ENGLAND**

The writer acknowledges support from Creative Scotland
towards the writing of this title.

ALBA | CHRUTHACHAIL

Cover design: Neil Astley & Pamela Robertson-Pearce.

Printed in Great Britain by Bell & Bain Limited, Glasgow, Scotland, on
acid-free paper sourced from mills with FSC chain of custody certification.

For A

THE
GAELIC GARDEN
OF THE DEAD

AND AS TO the letter itself, what is the origin from which it is? Not hard. From legitera, to wit, a name for a certain animal lair that dwells on the seashore [in litore] named Molossus, and whosoever sees the lair of that animal, to him is revealed knowledge without study.

Auraicept na n-Éces, The Scholar's Primer (7th century)

THREE OR FOUR students, at the University of Jena, in the attempt to raise a spirit for the discovery of a supposed hidden treasure, were strangled or poisoned by the fumes of the charcoal they had been burning, in a close garden-house of a vineyard near Jena, while employed in their magic fumigations and charms. Only one was restored to life: and from his account of the noises and spectres (in his ears and eyes) as he was losing his senses, it was taken for granted that the bad spirit had destroyed them.[...] the spirit of avarice and folly; and that a very noxious spirit (gas or *Geist*) was the immediate cause of their death. But he contended that this latter spirit was the spirit of charcoal, which would have produced the same effect, had the young men been chanting psalms instead of incantations...

SAMUEL TAYLOR COLERIDGE, *Aids to Reflection* (1825)

An anecdote from Braemar shows an interesting reversal of this theme, although the story has only been preserved in translation:

'The Baillie Mor hanged Inverey an' his sons on a tree before their ain door, and got his land for his trouble. Their peer auld mither was put out o' her sense by this cruelty, and in her raving madness she prophesied that the tree would be green when his tribe would be as landless and sonless as he had made her…she cursed the clan, and predicted their downfall in a Gaelic rhyme, one verse of which I have thus translated by a friend:

> This tree will flourish high and broad,
>   Green as it grows today,
> When from the banks o' tbonnie Dee
>   Clann Fhionnlaidh's all away.

JOHN GRANT MICHIE: *Deeside tales: or Men and manners on Highland Deeside since 1745* (1908)

[156.]
A twelfth I know: if I see in a tree
a corpse from a halter hanging,
such spells I write, and paint in runes,
that the being descends and speaks.

– *Hávamál, The Words of Odin the High One
from the Elder or Poetic Edda (Sœmund's Edda),*
tr. Olive Bray

I

GLADE
OF THE SKULL

AILM – PINE

I *First Witness: Sweetness of Fire*

I open with a mouth of burning coal,
burst from the bitter bone of my skull
so suicides will come down to drink.

Forespoken water, rubbed on astonished eyes
                              of the future,
scarred the horses with lovers' curses,
drew the wershness out of voices, whispered
into quenched ashes –

Love's eyes are colourless:
a motive for moving through underworlds.

Voice-walker, I open speech –

demolishing the Antonine Wall, Pictish scribes,
Latin scrawlings – I deciphered them all,
reminiscing on disappearance
of Roman legions in Caledonian forest
led by Picti into hazel thickets.

Those were true hieroglyphs,
a body language of human sacrifice:
the skeleton's articulate dust.

II *Second Witness: Ash Feòlach*

Wild tinder of bone,
young charcoal marrow.
Nemeton.

Bone char of sugar,
tendon pyre,

Black heather suffumigation.
I drown in smoke

Like the young centurion
who lit the char bone god –

His tree has shout,
His tree is raked in oak:

In historia vision
Est historia exspiravit –

The history of vision
Is the history of ghost.

III *Third Witness: Stauncher of Shade*

Will fire turn jealous of wood?
Wood be consumed by envious smoke?

Throat to spirit throat
I rose,
beheld my head bones cross-wise broken,
hung in the burnt flesh of morning.

Colourless bestiaries pant at my feet,
Temperatures rising, rust my face.

I taught my shadow to rest for a while,
to rest in the shade from the heat.

But shade is only the surface
it is cast upon made darker;
a saturation by shadow.
A mountain made blue by distance
when sleet climbs the pines. A haunting
by hue. Colour, expanse, accident,
temperatures of darkness seep
beyond that which keeps my gaze –
sight-locked time did not witness
terse tints my own shadow moved
therein double-crossing the spectrum
with additives of rowan, rainbow oil
of peat water, broken blackthorn –
this shadow cum silt reflection
surges and swills at the back of my throat.

Now water's fiery modulation, bottle filled flame-water,
finds the voice grain in the singer, rising up unto itself.

Pitched to the green horses' frenzy, fetlock
to fetlock. I fixed them up myself.
Horses, whose strong backs
boys stood upon. Roped still, for hanging.

I undo my eyes, my mouth, my coat.

DUIR – OAK

I *Psalm for Lightning*

Mine was the scent of undertaking,
though he was bound by sense to sight.

Quicksilver slides, eye to eye, querent:

how to rub or draw
from himself
wood's secret lens?

His young vision, through bruised mist tracking,
seizes distant grazers –

> white antlered,
> cropping dawn –

> stag looks up.

King in the moon-tide sun,
precisely four parts beaten:

salt in the hunger of fire,
can reform of itself
a thirsty temple

trespass scraped
from the stag's leg
can weigh and presage printing

lightning skins damp with fire,
but hoar oak is kept
by mistletoe

death blooms consular,
flourishing for solar water,
bursts into flight.

II *Psalm for Thunder*

Had he touched lightning's touch,
ryatus water, raising flower?

Unfurled,
smouldering ribbons rise,
escape.

A lucid glance twists in his hands
of finger borrowed arrow:
slightly sprung, quivering.

My shadow guided dusk to
him, watched night

run him down. The quickened heel,
death pulling back.

Behind the hooves, swerving herds
in centuries of deer dust turn –

one is always lost.

III *Psalm for Rain*

It could be a flash
of occultation.

To kiss grief's rough touch
and bleeding, wipe a damaged mouth.

Oracular quiver: in metallic scrape,
a pre-history of floating feather.

Lightning me into skeleton.
                    I am in drought.

EADHA – ASPEN

I *Salt Coronach*

Salt upon me, I was at his death.
What ate, gave reverence, what grief, gave devil.

> Lean scriptures pass
> > the salted plate of dew –

Who shall consume the Sin Eater's evil?

> > Salt-swollen coffin house,
> > belief eaters and feral prayer,
> > rising ash of wersh whispers,
> > on whitened lips of croft house elders.

Coffin joined, I speak in sleep.
Board on board, I take his weight.

I push the bruise around his face,
lower case, in blood.

His breath's damp stain
shrank on shroud to fade:

> > the mirror's swatch of time
> > new rent –

> > death a ceilidh,
> > birth a wake –

a trembling shield of shadow raised:
a measure in the glass, his gaze –

> > who died to watch the dead.

II *Snow Coronach*

The boy whose neck was clad in rope
for stealing a deer, has been cut down.

His eyes have rolled away from hope

      mind enveloped in the snow
          that clouds in drifts along the slope.

A salt wood within the mound,
a salt dusted wound.

His split lip cracked and white, catches
on its sister head, rubs a dry, crackling tune.

Licked, it bursts sparks that flock and burn,
spinning
on a dwindling thumb.

III *Sleep Coronach*

    Winter, you desert-eater −

      the colour of vision
      is the glade in your skull.

      First the history of pain,
      then histories of sleep begin.

          Now hear: in winter's whittled ear −
          I hold death's death within my own.

    Lightning struck, those skull innards burn.
    Utilised fire.

Who holds the span?

Volatu tardo –
the eyes slow down.

II

TESTIMONY
OF THE ROCKS

ONN – GORSE

I *Casgadh Fola*

Walking to the heartland of the Gaelic alphabet
where spirit multitudes sleep rough
among the bales of slaughtered wheat,
I drank my lover's blood.

Spirtle of fire! Spirtle of blood!
I vanquish bloods at the weeping of bloods!

I drink down death from my lover's wound –

clockwise when I swallow, dowses,
when I cry,
anti-clockwise.

The horses are weeping, coat to coat,
in shorn mirrors I wash in mud,
altanach, the mountain moss,
stanches my mouth.

A hymn to sob, my ragged heart, goes four hands deep.
At the open wound, my obedient horse grazes
on the fiercest cruor.

My dust horse of fine black wind,
my milk mare whose dun eye
rolls, my stallion of peat and gorse
rubbed on sores of knowledge.
Red foal fetlock beneath my tongue,
my powder blue stallion: paddocks
of heat rise from your field,
grey dusk my horse hath chawed
in excrement of sunbeam,
my pyramid horse of sweet cud rose,
my fresh skinned horse,
lying in a plot of rust:

     my wounded parts grow younger
     – stay younger –
     fresh released to air.

I overheard those murmuring horses
in our fast flowing river grave:

     a rag of lyres
     unstrung in the mud.

Foals grazed on stewed limpets,
     salted fetlocks, brackish lashes –
     a wind to strip the tail from stallions.

Molasses kelp helped to the fields
     where moonlight plunges milk, salt and loam,
     where the Neolithic temple turns

     plough blades sharpened on blackened chunks
        of demolished worship, stones ploughed
        and re-established: croft lintels

     assimilate altars, wax and prayer still
     mounted to stopper the ears
     of soil effigies.

Mares raced on rage, smashing
the breakers, raced on at high
                    temperature as if the night froth of the field

turned centuries' salt, chariot
races of still listening deities
                    tested, tried in the clinging peat.

I have stanched such horses
trained to shoulder the weight of the field
and, when the plough blade breaks,
                    to stand away from the god.

                    The sea washes up dead sharks
                    their muzzles open in decay
                    the field washes up live stones
                    their skins glowing geal.

                    And in the shark, a horse's femur
                    her slow plod curled, and in the stone
                    my young mind's fever, pulling
                    its rising temple homeward.

II *Molossus Legitera*

The cave is only bone,
and swelters at the ancestral tip.

Cruel wand, the cross sectioned whip
of knowledge and desire
inter-mated on a barb of fire.

Slaughter is a two-way danger,
sanded down by struggle's hope.

I cross-fire on stepping stone boats,
barques of grief and trustiness,
keep those cell-razed runes of thought,
divining cold dream matter
heap the lot on a marine bonfire,
its spark-crossed air searing sweat.

III *Ninth Wave*

When the sea smells of bleeding, lying on a pile of shifting bones,
I recall your ocean, a booming catacomb, washing in and out of stench,
mounding up
its wild collection.

I had it at my fingertips, picking at the salted bits
saline carrion, soaking glyphs, washed up on a sighing beach.

Air smother, salt smother, sand smother, brine smother
all recall her muliebrous voice, rising off the restless ocean.

My corresponding cry spatters
sticks, quenches rocks,
hissing on the bonfire shore,
runs the hoarse black cave,
rising up becomes the wind
and down again – but again

on salt shore stubble,
my wind-wounded shadow stumbles.

Echoless, when I swim
my root note a drowning wind,
blown across its grieving dream,
rising from a sweating ocean
where a froth of nightmare forms
on my deep sleeping sea.

HUATH – HAWTHORN

I *Book of Sand*

Desert ambler – the language of footprints
is a history of walking.

Shrub chaparral of bleached bones –
your deepest thought covered with thorns,
your smallest action, excited by air –

The language of movement, a passage of blows,
waning pillar of distant fire,
the torture-grove of deer is near and I am tired.

II *Book of Dung*

Young wolf cloot,
padding shy through desert thocht,
round the lyre, defecate.

Dung cries at night
on the fields, in the river.
It is sweltering.

I will glove my eyes,
I will hood my tongue.

I will make me a wolf lure
of crepuscular thorn.

III *Book of Stone*

Broken in,
I expulse a stone garden.

My sand-soaked eye, close to the grain,
finds itself awake again
but is hesitant, outside the dream,
to return.

My heart – the hardest
rock there is,
thorn alone would soften it –
powder white and
powder black punished

disperses its shadow
across dry sand.

STRAIF – BLACKTHORN

I *Ogham Confession*

Histories of speech assuage my sadness
when I am star-raved, dark.

O zodiacal tree of curse,
I was alive in the era of voice,
grown as moss on the skull of tongues.

In kindling bones of dead letters,
recollecting splintered speeches,
classing visions, classing fevers,
bewildering my own seasons,

I mouthed a cant of bitter thorn –
withering copse of wood-raved charm.

Argot's corpse.
Now, that copse is gone.

It made you cry, why?

The listeners sit and die.
Swarmed in grief, loud note the flies.

Tatterdemalion, curse eaten coat
on oldest thorn held, faltered and fell,

You slit my throat,
                              I spoke –

II *Glyph Confession*

On murmur-briar and roar-briar,
I landed preambular

snuffed the blackness from its star,
wily love throat, prick immure.

How long I sought laughter underwater,
where the lilies hiss.

I only rained blood of planets,
smattering wind, barbing sea mist.

My distaff is a wound rock of skin,
thorn-kindled skein of stone.

My voice a spindle, cultivating tears.
Flame squandered light, water floundered star,
gnashed lore. Glamour.

My hunting lands are growing slower:
Where song stands still, I speak in colour.

III *Rune Confession*

Long I talked the hunger grasses,
returned in thirst, a spittle wisp:
my thorn globe burnt in a northern cornfield,
first sphere of a world, scorched tongue tip.

Reflex man, I intoned ghost –
strand of hair caught on a corpse bier:
double helix about my voice box,
drawn through the hole of an absent pine knot –

Cinder-walker, ember-walker,
coal-walker. Co-walker, ashed on dream.
How fire wilts on me in runes.
Quell blade of the quarter-walker, unquiet my tongue.

Sediments of smoke, sediments of soot:
with sunken eyes, I lift my chin –
shadow-gatherer lurks at my throat,
old speech-walk tinder, rekindling.

III

NEMETON

NUIN – ASH

I *Pre-Cognition of Fire*

Histories of demon grow wild in the trees:
brusque kisses of black bud hiss.

Is it humankind's history,
the burning liquid of her eye?

Snow falls: white flame of tress.
Solders her back: long, ash rivulet.
She, conqueress, her cold clear flesh.

You, small snake, baked in shadows of distrust,
rioter among the tombs, coiled upon
such gentle fires and blew them
into dust.

For fire is made by striking air:

Odorous, malodorous,
you roast alive in a living forest
this vast wood of still green embers
unred, unsapped, sears your skin
in coalish, ashen, thin streaked branches.

Enlist! Enlist! You scrawl a wall and disappear.

                    All fires contain your hiss.

II *Cognition of Bone*

Hours sorrow tongues:
tha ceann dubh air ghealach an drasda.

And she stands, stroking time.
Snake sleeps in the cowl of her lip,
her shawl of hair, my old ash crown.

Mouth open, her hour
dowses for lightning.

No bashing blossom vigorous
kisses that black moon's harsh deliverance,
bitterly biting silence.

Her spike mouth, turned,
is done.
Witless winds of the wild
stray calm.

III *Retro-Cognition of Ash*

Snake is singing, striking lightning
through its scales,
turns to woman, finds her sob
on fruit of stump, the love crushed rock.

                A long time ago the nights turned and spoke,
                one by one,
                urging stillness, arguing for darkness –
                the same as we all hold in the mouth.

Was there something cured in her stare?
A boy-free skeleton, the history of desire.

I first saw the poisoner from behind her own shade
then their shadows combined

listless, non-combative.

And she stroked its glaze-eyed gluttony
in the glimmer skin of thought.

So the breath detains the shadow.
So the adder and the viper.
So the wisdom into serpent.
So the venom spitting blood.

TINNE – HOLLY

I *Dream Marrow*

His last impression made on wood
kick-water worked to the gut,
word worn on air, a slow tornado of flaring hair.

Necklet of twigs, thrash-frothed
                    foams his face, wet-lipped in woods,
                    whose long howl pulls

                                        at the root of death.

                                        I have seen his quickening expire,
                                        his damp ooze along the break;
                                        his quarantined fire, now man,
                                        now stag, become slit throat choir.

II *Flame Marrow*

He drank from the skull of a slaughter-hawk,
inducing a trance whose avian conference
flew nocturnal, burnt off ancient dream stubble.
Testing in the colour tree,
bashed his vision, slept in pallor.
His kilt of Egyptian linen,
red wine spilt in amulet ash,
his flint of fire sucked spark,
jewel-culler, flick of flame.
His lone blood beads take temperature's time,
he is hot, when distanced but come near, cool down.
His heat scented tears – no watchpoint complain.
His wrist, a blood cuff raised in pain –
they drew the longing out from him.

Spring burns in a holy star,
winter cools on the backs of the leaves,
flares in a green fire-wash of dream,
rubbed from the bark of an emerald calendar.

Not ruby, the inner flesh of bark,
bleeding coral, tourmaline,
rubbed between carnelian rings,
but the instinct of wood:

charred bones in the upper throat
of a mute hart:
bone char hieroglyphs smoke,
charcoal marrow of the hunt.

COLL – HAZEL

I *Carrion Oracle*

Awake, from a wild night's vision in dream –
a cloak upon me, I was at my death.

Birds fuse to damage bones,
like the head bones of my teeth.

Those artery carvers and wild carvers
of bone were my carrion, smelling rot
in the once sweet heart of the wood.

II *Charcoal Oracle*

> He who trembles, stuns.
> Hung from the tree of my own skeleton,
> the birds came in.

Hummingbird, honeyed heart feeder, syphoned my hurting heart's blood.
The night owl swooped on my cranium, chipping to my brain flesh.
My right hand gashed to ribbons by the slaughter-hawk, the night-raven.
The left eye in my head, punctured carefully by a wren.
As I stood in a blood-fall of pain, fizzing guts of tears and bloods of sweat,
I became a brutal angel stock.

> He who trembles, stuns.
> Boy of leaves,
> boy of spattered lettering.

A gold eaglet ripped my lip flesh, my shoulder blades were wrenched
by a swan, a desperate rook split my toes from bone. Ventricles unravelled
by the feeding lark opened leaking sacks of lung. From rectum to colon,

the snipe dragged my intestine to ground, scraping the sweet grains from
my duodenum. Liver was lifted into the trees, kidneys spread beneath
me, carpals, femurs, ulna and radius emerged into flight, sternum and ribs
extended wings of the vulture-feeder, a bloodied and fat smeared tongue
sliced with the remaining marks of teeth was severed by a gull, trailing the
oesophagus and first parts of my inner throat up into higher branches, my
genitals peeled and wrenched by a scrat were dropped by my liver at
my tarsus, piled up with a tibula and ear lobe. My scalp, pared by the owl
crossed my face in a wet shadow as my cheeks were stripped by the
urgent thrush. My sawdust mask bickered, shaved by vicious robins.

He who trembles, stuns.

I was revealed to pine trees in a ligament of bone, a thought-walking
skeleton, conscripted to eagle, strapped to gull. My raw red bone
hipped to the wind, scratched into tree hollow. A feathered skin,
fighting, feeding. This is fire, sprung out of water. This, a hemlock of
fire-shockled owls, howling in the gold spun dark. This, thawed within
the raw thorn tree, the cold spring nightingale entangling with song.

III *Echo Oracle*

Love, the heart devourer,
leans in to speak in tongues of flame –
flame that fleck fire upon us once again:

a chaos of cinders
is as forest in fable
and to dream must return.

Late in the echo,
I dreamt of nothing,
but the echo was the dream.

IV

SCHOOL OF THE MOON

QUERT – APPLE

I *Fool of Hours*

Here we have begun,
in the long drawn shadow of sacrificial man.

The history of the moon,
is the history of the sun:

> lunar boscage, solar boscage –
> slit throat the victim,
> staggers through meaning –
> at the moment of my death
> comes sense.

Would I prove myself in a moon-water pool?
Whose face would I reveal?

I part the leaves of disease,
stare through.

Gentle, oracular fool.

II *Rood of Hours*

The white hart caught in crabbed apple branches
tied with lucent cords of musk, whose antlers drop,
                thudding in the ancient dust,
                bounds free.

                He swells holly salt,
                at the cusp of escape,
                scattered on his bellowing chest
                whose blood drops are dew
                on milky, spermy mistletoe
                whose pearlescent berry juices glow
                trembling, constellar musk.

Young stag, fierce footed in the rusted thicket,
his bone bewildered antler tree
raises and lowers obediently,
ribbons of mist in the clouds of his breath,
lifts his light hoof-sprint set
in the mud-yoked fruit of an inverted heart.

III *Boy of Hours*

        I keep my dark cell tight

        to diurnal thought
        for the raw-skinned fawn
        in the raw-boned hind,

        at medial night, I decompose.

In my bliss,

whose racing pelts
raise sweat in my eyes,
pull curse from my bone,
box ache in my ribs,
whose bright colour rarely flares,
glimpsed at the dawn of dusk,

vulgaris.

The white cell to my right,
a lyre string plucked
monochrome.

In it I distil
this recurring disc of daylight.

IOGH – YEW

I *Arrow Speaks*

The voice path of the arrow
is the history of the bow.

Contrapposto splinters bone,
to cleave his hart skeleton –

my tongue slides down
the back of his throat,
my head and heart couple
in his gut –

by dint of flesh, he twists
me up: bone stretched metal into shapely flame,
shatters flint sparks arraying ligament,
arrow tips dipped in time
cause cease.

Once I tricked honey, glancing
off mud, travelled a year
in a mortal wound but now
take shelter in young stag bone,
thought walker, divining form.

He takes me, trenched, close
to heart. My socket flight his
now dead eye, spilt upon
its universe.

Are the distant glints of stars,
arrowheads aimed at us?

Flesh in flesh we turn and grin,
from an undergrowth of starlit bone.

These voice shot paths
burst into bodies fallen backwards
a lightning field of white hot corpses
stripped, those stars, of their dying conscience
skeletal ore, stellar coppice,
the language of flight, heavy with losses –

Night cropped, I have spoken
in the graveyard of the stags.

Now my living tongue, buried
in his buried flesh, has slowly
climbed through root and worm,
my stubborn head moves his head,
toward the emerging yew
that from his skull grows rooted,
futile – seeking anew
the living bow:

the voice path of the arrow
is to kill.

II *Poison Speaks*

Dule toxicon, eve of poison,
this night I dream of swallowing ice,
of love's voice cast on black water,
in lunar festoons of ice-barked water
cracking in lone yew trees at midnight in the Hebrides.

The moon nurses these longbow boughs,
creates her silver, encouraging milk
berried in each young yew's blood.

I am tinted with her praise, a blood-dip
embroiled in fruit; a malnourished paradise.

My poison thought rays straight from shoot
to course this hopeless compass,
filling artery with forest.

III *Bow Speaks*

Barbaric bowl of bone, its roar is white.
Memory water, frozen contempt.

Milk sours on the old sundial.
The moon devours love's rotting carcass.

Those sucking eyes kiss,
the turned disc holds its breath.

I scrape moonlight off like sweat,
and die in the attempt, strigilis.

BEITHE – BIRCH

I *Sand Mirror*

Alone in my mirror, I saw centuries bitter
come down to pasture for the Highland winter

and late in the charm garden, thought of my mother,
pulling at her book, like cooling meat.

Who thought she could read it?

In the air nothing,
but the sound of winter
where the whirlwind lies in ice.

Now, old coronach, she is keening in her sleep.
Sleep distended sleep, distended sleep, distended –
late in the woods, I came to find her weep:

I speak from lids of lowered eyes,
conjoined with black fire on fire
by day their seams are sodden,
seeping.

Eyes of birch, flake on flake,
moulting winter sight.

II *Bark Mirror*

Night perceives more clearly
than all other senses, requiring that we look direct,

daylight's mirrors, rubbed to weariness,
merely receive their evidence.

So survival by the shadow, a sense in time,
wrests place.

This presage of a charm of a dial
by daylight fades, by night becomes night itself.
Lifted, lifts.

Corresponding sights evince.

As this night I touch the quickened hind,
garlic tipped in lightning.

A flame to sense
will bring back speech.

She will speak from the hanging tree,
a fire prayer of aerial burial –

Will you come, or will you go,
or will you consume the wild hart's shadow?

III *Fire Mirror*

The history of the living
is the history of the dead.

The skull has flared,
guttered, died.

The tongue intoned
truth in lies.

Time has darkened
in a voice.

We are death's own
suicide.

NOTES

I GLADE OF THE SKULL

AILM

In the Highlands, the pine was sometimes used as a hanging tree, and this one relates to a hanging tree in Braemar which is still wired up to remain standing.

'burst from the bitter mouth of my skull / so suicides will come down to drink': a reversal of the early, macabre folk medical cure for epilepsy which was to prescribe water drunk from the skull of a suicide.

Feòlach is 'fleshy, meaty' carnage, slaughter'.

'the water's fiery modulation' taken from a Gypsy charm against the evil eye; 'as the incantation was sung, a bottle of water was being filled and the performer so modulated his voice as to chime with the gurgling of the liquid as it poured into the vessel. The incantation (*eolas a' chronachaidh*) Against nine slender fairies...' Mr Leland – Gypsy Sorcery – 'a jar filled with water from a stream and it must be taken.'

EADHA

Fé, or measuring sticks for corpses were made from aspen.

Salt was applied to a corpse, resting on the chest, in Highland funeral ritual – thought to absorb excess moisture.

A Sin Eater was a man who would be paid by a family to consume the sins of the deceased in the literal form of food – often bread and cheese, alongside ale, that had been placed on the chest of the corpse. Shunned by their local communities, Sin Eaters were tolerated by the church and performed a special duty, especially in cases of suicide.

'Death a ceilidh, birth a wake', refer to a pernicious traditional Gaelic belief that celebration was to be made at the death of an individual, now that they were proceeding to the happiness of heaven but that mourning was necessary on the birth of a child for the life of woe they were about to lead.

II TESTIMONY OF THE ROCKS

TESTIMONY OF THE ROCKS

Borrowed from Hugh Miller's geology title.

ONN

Casgadh Fola or Staunching Blood. The belief is that some Highlanders had the ability to staunch blood. Horse gelders were supposed to be particularly skilled in this art.

Fierce blood. *An troma-laidhe* was a charm against nightmare.

The 'ninth wave' is traditionally the wave you drown in.

STRAIF

A 'reflex man', as defined by the Rev. Robert Kirk in his *Secret Commonwealth of Elves, Faunes and Fairies* is another term for the co-walker or Highland double.

III NEMETON

NUIN

There is a Gaelic saying 'the snake will go through the red blazing fire rather than through the leaves of the ash'.

TINNE

'Charcoal marrow', an old phrase for Holly.

IV SCHOOL OF THE MOON

QUERT

'slit throat the victim / staggers through meaning' refers to the druidic practise of divination through the way a sacrificial victim fell after his throat was cut.

IOGH

It is commonly understood that the severe dearth of Yews in the British countryside and their preservation in church-yards might well correspond to the mass production of yew bows during the middle-ages for use in warfare.

BEITHE

Gypsies assert that lightning leaves behind it a smell like garlic.

RETRO-COGNITION

In his conclusion to the abridged version of *The Golden Bough*, James George Frazer notes 'tradition ran that the fate of the Hays of Errol, an estate in Perthshire, near the Firth of Tay, was bound up with the mistletoe that grew on a certain great oak. A member of the Hay family has recorded the old belief as follows: 'Among the low country families the badges are almost generally forgotten; but it appears by an ancient MS, and the tradition of a few old people in Perthshire, that the badge of the Hays was the mistletoe.' Frazer goes on to describe how the life of the Errols of Hay was traditionally bound up with the mistletoe that grew extensively on a great oak in the district and quotes Thomas the Rhymer:

> While the mistletoe bats on Errol's aik,
> And that aim stands fast,
> That Hays shall flourish and their good grey hawk
> Shall nocht flinch before the blast.
>
> But when the root of the aik decays,
> and the mistletoe dwines on its withered breast,
> The grass shall grow on Errol's hearthstane,
> And the corbie roup in the falcon's nest.

As a meta-narrative for the Gaelic alphabet of trees or the Irish tree Ogham currently in use in Scotland, Frazer's seminal clarification of the retainer – the mistletoe – as a receptacle for the life-force of the language itself when faced with constant demise, remains a tenacious motif. The binary descriptions of living and dying are never far behind most contemporary discussions of Scottish Gaelic which seems to have chosen the Sanskrit term 'para desa', the high lands or paradise in which to co-walk itself as both living and dead, as an off-shoot or graft of the flourishing Irish root form. This peripheral grip suggests the importance of the edges of the matter, that Gaelic in Scotland must now crucially occupy the peripheries of cultural consciousness, whilst still lodged firmly at the centre. Here I quote from *The Burning Tree: Poems from the First*

Thousand Years of Welsh Verse, selected and translated by Gwyn Williams (1956):

> '...A tall tree on the river's bank, one half of it burning from root to top, the other half in green leaf.'
> – Peredur son of Efrawg

Matthew Arnold in his *Study of Celtic Literature* notes a passage from the *Mabinogion* as an instance of what he calls Celtic magic. 'And they saw a tall tree by the side of the river, one half of which was in flames from the root to the top, and the other half was green and in full leaf.' It was enough for Arnold to recognise this as magic, distinguishing it from the radiant, uncomplicated Greek way of handling nature, without prying into the mechanics of the image. [...]

The absence of a centred design, of an architectural quality, is not a weakness in old Welsh poetry, but results quite reasonably from a specific view of composition. English and most Western European creative activity has been conditioned by the inheritance from Greece and Rome of the notion of a central point of interest in a poem, picture, or play, a nodal region to which everything leads and on which everything depends. The dispersed nature of the thematic splintering of Welsh poetry is not due to a failure to follow this classical convention. Aneirin, Gwalchami, Cynnddelw and Hywel ab Owain were not trying to write poems that would read like Greek temples or even Gothic cathedrals but, rather, like stone circles or the contour-following rings of the forts from which they fought, with hidden ways slipping from one ring to another. More obviously, their writing was like the interwoven inventions preserved in early Celtic manuscripts and on stone crosses, where what happens in a corner is as important as what happens at the centre, because there often is no centre.

Robert Graves might agree with this kind of formal categorisation when citing lunar and solar types of poetic thought; 'the history of English poetry has been the modifying of the original moon-poetry, which is stressed, with sun poetry (intellectual, Apollo poetry) which is measured in regular beats and measures'.

But where does this leave our discussion? To be tipped in moonlight starts to sound like the Celtic Twilight works of writers such as the shape-shifting William Sharpe/Fiona MacLeod. Most Gaelic writers today would prefer the sun-soaked slopes of Duncan Ban MacIntyre's 'In Praise of Ben Dorain'. Derick Thomson refers to some Scottish Gaelic bardic verse and praise poetry that 'showing technical competence but no lyrical fire, can be impressive although they do not move the reader.' His astonishing description of an anonymous elegy for Sir Norman MacLeod of Bernera, likens its structure to formal death duties: 'its long series of monosyllables, like earth trickling onto a coffin-lid, can be physically observed'. Here again, we find a rhetoric of death entering into a formal discussion of Scottish Gaelic poetry.

Two scholastic traditions in the Highlands of Scotland suggest a lunar tendency; one, named 'the School of the Moon', trained its students in the fine art of cattle rustling and, so-called, needs not much further explanation except that it is better to perceive this seemingly roguish practice in relation to the 'coup d'état' as a kind of territorial game – an enlarged version of chess with the landscape as the board. Then we have the more enigmatic bardic training in composition which involved spending the span of a day lying down in a darkened cell, before rising to spend the night in writing. It suggests not only succinct mnemonics but a performative premonition of what was subsequently to be written. Why lying down? Why not walking, as so many writers do to compose? Why during the day, locked away from sunlight? Why in a cell? Why to emerge not the following day but that night? Secret arts... dark arts. It is tempting to perceive this apparent shut-down of the body with only the instincts, spirit and intellect of the imagining mind operational as a simultaneity of living and dying – an experience in which the individual composed out of his life and his death as twin allies. The iambic foot hovers and disappears. The whole of the spine is laid out, if the poet is on his back. If lying facedown, perhaps the heart heard more within ribs actively pushing and releasing, rising and falling, to slightly raise and lower the body whose breath left a small hot place on hessian, on stone, on wood... 'since they sewed the shroud over your mouth'. The dream chamber might include sonic sweet spots where breath became tanta-mount to the sound of a storm, or the heart beat a pacing

animal. Might there be a small opening for a long protuber-
ant finger of sunlight to travel down directly to the poet's
temple to indicate the sacrificial blade, the stylus, the point
of the whip, the point of the third eye? Could this be at mid-
day? Or did darkness enable the writer to forget his physical
body – 'as the image melts into the notion of tree, so does
the tree pass into that of image'.

*   *   *   *

Sir Thomas Innes of Learney observed 'no more can one
believe that floral badges would be of any value as cognisance
in battle. They are probably symbolic flowers or tribal charm
plants.' Expanding on this history of twisted clan badge roots
we find:

> The 'Researches' of Mr Davies have thrown much light on
> Celtic Antiquities, and in his pages will be found several passages
> from bardic compositions, which elucidate the tree system of
> learning. It is well known that various trees and shrubs have
> been symbolical, or used as tokens, but the learning of the sprigs
> consisted in arranging, tying, and intertwining them in various
> ways, thereby altering their expression or import. There is a
> work which Mr Davies quotes, in which the author says 'he
> loves the sprigs with their woven tops, tied with a hundred
> knots, after the manner of the Celts, which the artists employed
> about their mystery'. Small branches of different trees were
> fastened together, and being 'placed in the tablet of devices,
> they were read by sages who were versed in science'. The art
> of tying the sprigs in numerous and intricate knots was an
> important part of the mystical studies of the druidical order,
> and appears to have been known by few. Taliesin, who gloried in
> belonging to the profession, boasts of this part of his knowledge;
> his acquaintance with every sprig, and the meaning of the
> trees, he calls 'understanding his institute'. We thus see that
> the Celts had a method of conveying their knowledge to the
> initiated by a sort of hieroglyphic, or symbolical character,
> produced by twigs, or branches of various trees, and the char-
> acters which afterwards formed an alphabet, represented those
> branches and retained the names of different trees. I shall now
> draw the reader's attention to the representations in ancient
> sculpture of these intricate, but, at one time, significant com-

binations and interlacings, from whence, I conceive, is to be deduced a style of ornament that was long retained, not only by the Gael, but by others, without knowing to what origin it was to be referred.

*   *   *   *

One of the words for forest in Gaelic – *coille* – begins with a hazel tree (c – *coll*), followed by a furze or spindle (o for *onn/ oir*), a yew (i for *iogh*), two rowans (l – *luis*) and an aspen (e – *eadha*). Unsurprisingly, these comprise some of the most potent symbolic magical trees in the Gaelic alphabet. Pliny says the optimum time to fell trees is when there is a lunar conjunction with the sun, defined as the interlinium or the moon's silence. It is a fine point of debate to argue whether poetic trees invoked are felled or seeded when pronounced. To have the presence of trees attending every word, constantly situates the language, its listeners and speakers within an overwhelming forest, covertly degrading meaning apart from the shadow of each oak, ash and elm whilst simultaneously banning or refusing to register others such as the beech. The images of each tree in itself, then, sprang from a symbolic intent. This co or code-dependency gives rise to complex and subtle vegetal kennings in the history of early Gaelic poetry. It may be that the presence of the clan badge, only lightly touched on by Victorian writers, engaged mostly with the complexities of tartan and its own language. Yet indigenous dye culture in the Highlands, though impacted on by sophisticated imports of substances such as cochineal, still found its plants locally. The leaf, root, flower and branch of many plants could form a sub-strata of associative meaning through wish, waulk and charm culture present within the making and staining of cloth, with the over-arching implications of a forested mode of communication. Badge of plant, tongue of tree –

Lament for Alasdair of Glengarry

Bu tu 'n t-iubar ás a' coillidh,
Bu tu 'n darach daingeann láidir,
Bu tu 'n cuileann, bu tu 'n droigheann

Bu tu 'n t-abhall molach bláthmhor;
Cha robh meur annad den chritheann,
Cha robh do dhlighe ri feárna:
Cha robh do cáirdeas ri leamhan –
Bu tu leannan nam ban álainn.

You were the yew from the forest,
you were the strong and steadfast oak,
you were the holly, you were the blackthorn,
the knotted, blossomed apple.
You had nothing of the aspen,
owed nothing to the alder,
had no friendship for the elm;
you were the darling of beautiful women.

SILEAS NA CEAPAICH

These badges or *suaicheantas* were perhaps like the Golden Bough – the spirit of the man or of the clan either kept in it or as a carrying receptacle in case of death in battle; a place for the spirit to retreat to and very powerful as a metonymic device – i.e. one sprig denoted the whole nature of the oak; the property of 'oak'. Shakespeare was aware of this in his ominous Birnam Wood that seems to move towards Macbeth, which is essentially an army of enlarged sprigs – a battalion of branches. John MacInnes, discussing the panegyric code in Gaelic poetry, states 'the kenning most commonly involved is that of the tree or the forest and the image of the wounded sapling or of the tree of the forest stripped of its foliage occurs throughout the elegiac poetry'. One of two remaining trees of Birnam Wood is an ancient oak. It is tempting to perceive Shakespeare as utilising the royal Stuart badge of the oak leaf as a force of destruction in combating Macbeth's instinct as the play was composed for James VI; a Stuart king. This would be the temporarily healthy symbol, the thriving tree kenning, turned to make man suffer as opposed to the wounded tree metaphor but, as Frazer muses, all kings die in the end.

*   *   *   *

If Scottish Gaelic is still curated by trees, perhaps it is possible that the spirit of the language might be said to be held or kept within the trees themselves. Struck by lightning, an oak will burn from the inside out for a long time before burning out. The co-walker of the oak is the mistletoe, as already pointed out – the royal oak, the bardic mistletoe. It may be that the survival of Scottish Gaelic which interminably shadows its own demise, forces it to operate – true to form – in a metaphoric moonlight. The solar conditions of king slaying king; system slaying system by oppressor and oppressed, don't quite resolve when overlaying the history of Scottish Gaelic language culture and the English language. It is tempting to situate the essence – the life force of the language – within something like the mistletoe, however. That, perforce, the magical vegetable imprint of and on each letter collapses Gaelic back into a language of leaves. This is not to say it does not matter. It is perhaps more about the possibility of the Gaelic language remaining as spoken before humans, in the sounds of the wind in branches, where it will be still after. That the symbol of tree is to indicate a language comprised of tree itself, beyond the centre of human utterance.

A CRISIS OF DREAM

WITNESS: CONSPIRACY OF TRUST

EXECUTION

Roaring fire

A gentle beheading in flame.
WEEPNOMORE

TERROR

OAK STAIRCASE
OAK STAIRCASE
OAK STAIRCASE

OAK STAIRCASE
OAK STAIRCASE
OAK STAIRCASE
OAK STAIRCASE

<u>TOMB</u>

TOMB

Tomb

tomb

TOMB
Laminates of gold
Kneeling dagger

Hawk kneeling dagger

WHITE STAG

St. Giles Cathedral
Edinburgh

UNDERGROUND
CITY

TAPHOS

The white stag strung like a lyre

Harp star hanging from the vulture

clutched in its falling claws

King David plucks his golden strings

string

His pulsed head piled on lyres

strings

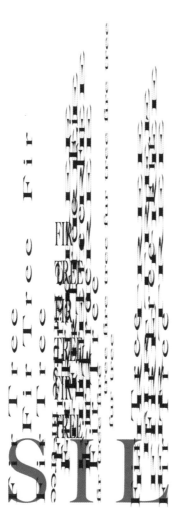

Fir Tree Tree Tree

Fir Tree Fir

FIR TREE FIR TREE FIR TREE

SILENCE

TURNS LOOKS

native kneeling

naked flank

knife

(68) nin gi'katch ja'igwa

Looks only

I

should have been killed

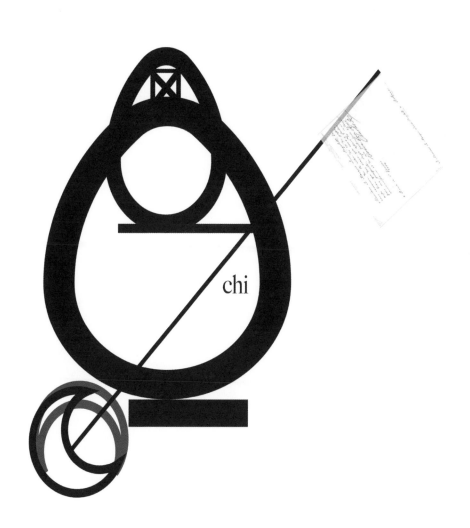

chi

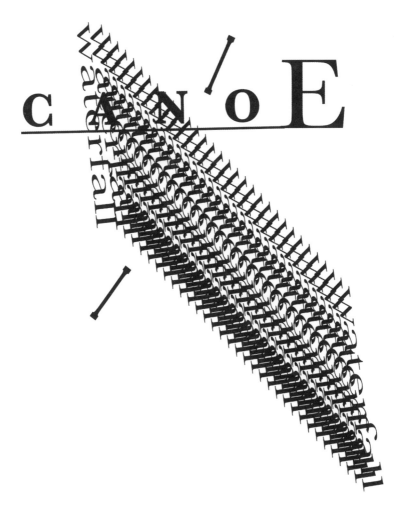

wild nowe...

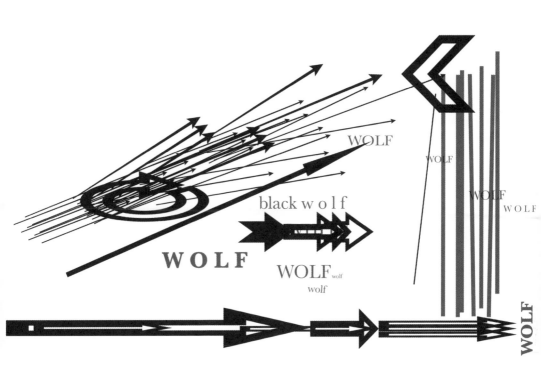

WOLF

black w o l f

WOLF

WOLF wolf

wolf

WOLF

WOLF

WOLF

WOLF

WOLF

organs of the teeth

constellar tenacity

HE DIED SHE DREAMED IN THE DESERT

IN THE END IS MY BEGINNING

35 DESTROYED SONNETS TO MARY QUEEN OF SCOTS

Dedicated to Anthony Slessor,
twelfth great grandson of Mary Queen of Scots.

I

THE DESCENT

But time…being made of steel and rust
Turns snow and silk and milk to dust.

SIR WALTER RALEIGH

35

Punctured! Dissatisfactions of the bow:
Who ploughs at night the grim sagittal course
to chart the arrow's blood-swiftening force
I ask for my heart, that you aim below
fast quickening ribs whose breath falls shallow
and sweat-wet fingertips' delicate trace
along the lips of my maidenhead's face
which, before the blade, love's death made sallow:

or reverse your course to shift the stellar sand –
my stars made indifferent to my self,
inconsiderate of heart conjured stealth
pinioned by your flashing code: guiding blood
spilled by star-worked pen, executioner's hand
shoots the night-worked arrow, misunderstood.

This sheaf of papers, comet ridden, is restless.
As if light within light, the original sin
begotten of itself, sheds its skin –
so your fingers flex, still working the jess
for the signature you have hawked, Good Bess.
You scrawled in sour lemon, a fire sermon
emerging in heat flushed secret, a merlin
that hovers, feverish in your caress.

Such birds explode to light, that fire again
redoubled in the inkwell's stormy flight
I saw the tri-fold meteor spluttered from your pen,
burst into a fine feathered ghost tonight
a three-score phoenix god scribed your amen
into the sky of my waking dream, quills alight.

I dreamed of a sawdust chandelier
whose crystals were drops of driftwood dredged
from all the world's shipwrecks: god's figurehead,
and it swung, as I dreamt, ever closer to my fear,
softly releasing sweet incense into the clear,
black night air, as that great barge carries the dead,
but instead of my death, it passaged my dread
and the water it ploughed comprised of one tear.

Great smouldering barque, your figurehead sings
into the dark, the death song of queens, of kings,
over sea birds that circle like faint rings of smoke,
your floating lamp burns, as a lighthouse brings
death to itself: you are moth and flame both –
so lamp lights my dread of shade, performs two killings.

32

No fire-traiked garden forced my soles to run;
the mud-hot ground went coldly in my wake
I left it there; a scarf cooled at night-break,
no solar burn had made me move; but moon,
foreshadowed, gave the day its low rune
and made the flowers pant as the deer run:
lick salt left on my skin from sweated sun,
pant to the stars in their silver-streaked tune.

My night has paused among the flowers, stunned.
Configured icicles cling to caress
as heat creates cold, if boiling numbness;
as flowers would pause, sunless, to open –
retain their own heat if by heat undressed
as I myself stall in heart-heat benumbed.

31

Did you tear open a mirror last night?
Poor envelope of star-littered action;
I open my mouth; with diamond diction,
scratch the pane of your pain: crystalline slight;
sleight of hand so hard to smack the sky's sight
now the tears that smart are my falling stars,
the heart-torn mirror ripped on soundless wars
as soundless my tears on the glass alight.

Look you! Is prison a safe destiny?
Do you bombaze – just as I am amazed
at my wrists' charm bracelets' intensity?
So star-shackled, my pen has diamond razed
– and failed – to cut your quick of verity.
You strike my mirror and I am death grazed.

bombaze: amaze.

I made an impression; my ring on wood,
as wood itself renews rings with age,
and descended down this wood: a stair stage
like the stage, ringed with men, for my death-hood.
This arena was made for their own good,
for mine has been stripped, revealing white sap
beneath scarlet bark, the corpse's mishap,
for reaped in the wood, death my ring has wooed.

You did not find any time in my ring,
my corpse-copse grew up straight, pressing air – earth,
my end is my beginning; death my birth,
collapsed the way the axe reveals the sap
in a sudden gash that fixes the girth,
prevents sparkling rings of truth from outward rippling.

29

I – the wildest beast in my bestiary,
unstitched, yet stitched in a weary prison,
chamber of my boredom's terrorism,
needled into eden's ark; unwordly
muffled in the cloth, graffiti scurry:
hanging by a thread, circus magician
coupled catholic, protestantism;
double-headed beast, taboo votary.

I sew them all into their rebel skins
furred, fleshed and scaled within the cotton's scope
or lazing, flicking flies from silk's slim rope,
or frayed with hope from woodland tapestry,
here the lion, here the hare's twisted lope,
here my paw, as of Eve's bestial sins.

28

When treading boards of splintered wood I pray
not for my punctured foot but for the tree
whose sudden, gifted pain my hurt can see
more clear than if I were in a wooded play
or at hunt brought me down a bird a day,
brittle twig clutched in its dying talon,
that scraped my hand a bright vermilion,
no: ask for the wood's execution stay.

I will not damage sapling nor linnet,
unless broken by death's hapless visit –
tis built for them, as much for me, minute
by minute over days three, exquisite
pain in my ear; scaffold's torture in it –
young trees torn down, my life to deposit.

I heard you hung my severed hand in air,
that I was handled Ethiopian,
that my courting life was deemed fallopian,
linked with abortive dreams of fortune 's dare –
dreams interlinked with cut fingers fair.
And from dream you removed into vision;
and from vision skirted straight derision,
but you have the queen's mantle, worn with flair.

Yet I am a queen who dresses alone;
my throne has not cooled yet, neither my glass
clothed in visions, I dream yet of my crown
lying sweet on my lawn, my dried, sweet grass
a cool white forehead on a calm spring morn,
is wiped by death's hand, that fast freezing blast.

26

What is it to be acutely free? A man
weighed before war, returns from war deadweight
eyes lined with lead, a scar-red mouth in paint
makes his accurate likeness disintegrate, faint
trace of a smile on his lips, his own hook-caught bait –
his people make the scales his mirror – a flesh ikon
the hidden match, his pyre's suggestion;
my likeness – same – is watermarked in flame.

My line was always taught to fish itself;
to execute its own image of death –
it is always in the mouth, we surrender breath
and so I made myself like unto myself.
But then you came, intervened. A dead loss
in my double; freely caught in my life game.

25

Bricked Sebastien licks his wounds, sewer bound,
pricked with shafts and arrow heads, twitching limbs, like his,
by death, my bones are used as trophies
and flail to beat the patterned god pulse – pound –
longing to martyr one of their deaths found
at either end – since birth has been dead twice
seen as life, ground in its own ransom price:
charred, stoned, beaten, flogged, hanged, beheaded, drowned.

Fearing flame, I fire mine from the shoulder,
death staggers, falls, expulses stars – a universe –
slow darkening sand, theatre's histories –
lie juddering, grounded, growing colder,
I quiver my arrow, as birth through me whispers
close now to death; 'I use your bones as trophies'.

24

'Or if you sometimes have wished' you could take back
what you said about my mouth of rubies, pearls
and gentle breath, for sometimes the deepest words lack
what I myself find confused within my selves –
the ones, so far, I now am constructed of
that reach you, not in person, but by letter.
Perhaps really, you would find a pensive mouth
and all the brooding more, by brooding better –

Do you not think your France would have bettered
the little flame haired girl who danced with birds,
who now by her own hand, perhaps, has fettered
her like-minded self: one of gold woods wild?
For I am not self possessed but seem to choose
men – and love – Ronsard, for whom I always lose.

2 3

If salt were snow it would season my dreams
with the flavour of fear, cover my tracks
if ever-wild endeavour, dreaming lacks –
though snow melts, salt stays to weather extremes.
Now run harder, my dual saline streams,
streaked in heat, falling dream, nakedness backs
like the fallen snow the woman attacks,
flesh-melted flakes, seasoned bare bone redeems.

Fallen like the hunted tear's temperature,
cooled, though partly warmed on my weathered face
moves through crystalline ice to end its race
as cold rock-face salt just as gleaming snow
glitters at high altitude; cold tears trace,
tears that salt my dreams' glacial venture.

Dead wood; the night-jar grips, wersht, shaved, moon-burnt,
chrysalis of nascent, trembling diamond:
necklace of dense compression: imprisoned
stars haunt the lesson the night equips, earnt
through bars of distilled death-lights – that gripped – weren't
softened: metal shafts, shining time's pinions
whose flight, whose talons, my needle's minions,
punctured on the gleaming shaft, stasis learnt.

And stasis too, my grave adamantine,
pocked indifference met the mark's station:
compression of a stony complexion,
solemn weight of tearful hour-glass glistens
a diamond set in its own commission:
star-chawed when severed from my sparkling spine.

Fire-addled marigold, the dusk-lake spreads
like wild-fire swift on growing death of sleep –
twin stars, twin flower heads, from darkness seep
from love's skull pan firing bright arrowheads:
hot blooms laid on life and death: those newlyweds
hot dissolution, my eyes: star-worked pools
hot eviction! – night slowed – one arrow cools,
splits the second weapon's shaft, twin thoroughbreds.

My eyes, both mutineers, collapse on sight:
belligerent meteors – dead red stars
red clarity; bewildered universe,
red curse of sudden youth, compelled by doom's
red-tressed, stellar blooms that from dark disperse –
marigolds fading from the sun's young light.

20

My cell has pressed me down; mouth of diamond:
I chew heaven backwards in my queen sleep,
teeth ground so hard – like eyes – they seem to weep,
and pawning my skull, create an island
of blood-bickered dream; a ground horizon.
This mouth of tears, all emotion wizened
is hard to swallow, though I am seasoned
within my life's treason to be frightened.

It is hard to see with a jewelled tongue –
I lie and scourge the pelts of old nightmare
probe their furred depths like a young stallion,
loose the stirrups, the straps; saddling nowhere
but for death, in sparkling life's rebellion,
my words – like a diamond bit – now ensnare.

19

Death's skeleton, riding, rose dust to dust,
grows ash scented gardens; lovers' compost,
fills with lunar tension; dark liquids lost,
dawn's delicate climate, breaking night's trust;
is love-flushed with violence, passion blooms' rust.
His bones are beguiled by witchcraft of flesh;
or star-craft of lies, a spiritual mesh,
that quizzes, that clings, though all stars combust –

I stand amazed that he hazards his blade
his silver-haired maiden offering him
no slight reflection, no hovering shade,
in the metal slice mirror, empty, slim,
only motes of dust, compression has made
of the language of death, love has made dim.

18

My lord, you were posted in this valley,
like Samson, eyeless in his framed, lost strengths
but unlike him you are not shorn; great lengths
of matted hair chain you: slave to galley:
withstanding exercise, your wits won't tally.
At least the ship-slave has his aching boat,
will drown in keeping his muscles afloat
but you are, to pole, tethered totally.

I know you have survived at half your size:
senses seized; doubled over in the mud.
I know your pole is animal disguise;
you feel it pulse against your heartbeat's thud
but you are still my slave within my eyes,
whose dim Samson tears are seas of love's flood.

17

Charcoal of dreams; love's long, dark compression,
is pressed from the bloodlines of my pulped heart.
Veinous the vineyard, trodden sweetly tart –
draw from it a diamond; crushed obsession,
brilliant young fruit; the garden's temptation –
the snake's glass eye revolves in its socket
and I am like Eve, one fruit I pocket,
stolen from my diamond-hidden lesson.

For is it not like Iscariot's kiss
the necessary betrayal of jewel?
She is not so hard a diamond mistress –
my heart or the one I attempt to steal.
I am her pressing gem, now testing Bess,
she is my hardened kiss, drawn – disloyal.

16

My troubled troubadour; they dealt your card
your voice, your hunch, your Italian guitar –
too much, your lute, your confidence bizarre
(though professionally warned by stars), bard;
they thought my royal reputation marred.
Yet do not desist your evening visit –
does a sparrow, fruit, resist to plummet?
As ghost you stand in the killers' orchard.

Queene fruits fall, decay, to seed the tree
but when you fell from me, my tree was torn
limb from limb; your knife-spry execution
provided no note to pin to your life
save the recurring blood-stain I will mourn,
cherry red tears pollinate my queene, bee.

Queene: the name of an Elizabethan apple.

15

Removing my heart, he perspired a kind
of dreamless mist for conscience, for hindsight,
wet with the kind of haar of my first alight
and kind on kind, of nothing came my mind
a type of seed, peeled from usual rind,
pearled with the morning's dew-teared plight
when facing dawn without the skin of night,
my heart met his mind, but sense did not find.

As the brume fast peels away from the sea,
as the bells peel for the newly made dead,
as a last repeal, I am stripped back from me
like the blood on the hymen split sheet read
as proof of the wedding night, my heart plea
proved nothing but its own fulfilling dread.

14

Son; I am reigned in fast falling tears,
I know there are many stairs from boy to manhood –
though I know not how to climb them, I understood
how you found your first footing in my labours,
the soft-caul curtain hung across flesh frontiers
treading constellation, as fast falling stars would,
if struggling for breath, if returning to light could
illuminate the delicate trace of their fears.

But I cannot hold you close, cannot rein you in –
you will be tethered on straps of greater leather
by culture's birth, not mother's; fashioned for a king.
But I would not you restrain; boy of the heather,
where the wild thistle stars the water's weeping –
guide you to myself with slight touch of a feather.

13

I see that it is snowing in my tomb
and that now the salt-lick deer come down
to tongue the many sorrows time will drown,
to generate a thirst in death's new room.
My mineral bone, stag and dog consume,
lap up potassium from my red gown,
suck the marrow from my now headless crown,
take up nutrition from my new-sealed womb.

In deer, I fix transubstantiation;
locking horns to grapple with young stag tongue –
come to suck my fear, young winter's children
suckle my limbs – into Christ I have sung;
nibble the hide I wore for my nation,
lick me into legend I have begun.

1 2

Just as my violet complexion keeps
twilight pallor in grief – not dark, nor light
but visible as by owls at night,
to those who stalk it; nocturnal steeps
but the owl eye never seals when he sleeps:
not resting nor waking, a limbo-sight,
the dusk of his dawn, a fixity fight,
so my face is fixed pale by hot-cold weeps.

But pallor as locked in a moon by sun,
can only be realised in cool contrast –
her gold summer net splits: silver tears run
that only seem true in cold lunar blast
just as winter the summer has outdone,
always pale, my face shows: nothing can last.

11

Arriving in fog in a listing boat,
astraea's dirge, for me, in my reluctant barge,
in sin's fair dream, lacking vision's luggage
a non-fairie queene, fixed in a moat
the castle-mirage, drowning afloat –
a premature Ophelia, swimming in blood,
belligerent Duessa, waiting for the flood –
I alighted on my death, changed my life-dipped coat.

As otter changes pelt, as stag shreds his velvet,
I shape-shift all my haunts from France onto Scotland.
Yet Scotland in itself shall reshape by hand
the Queen in its flesh, the ourgilt shame,
pray on the silver stern at her command,
just as winter takes the cloak of the leveret.

fog: moss; *listing:* wishing; *dirge:* office for the dead; *ourgilt:* tinged with gold; *pray:*
prey; *stern:* stars.

10

Snow-plashed blood: scattered, fire-soaked wood,
I wear Christ's crown of the wild blackthorn
but unlike the lion's splinter, have no Jerome.
Dead Rood, Holy Rood – the stag has understood;
budding late, like the hart's thought, budding rude,
carpentry makes a sudden sea from loam;
finds the only nerve within the dry bone,
makes the child to its murderer understood.

When suddenly pursued by the fast panting dark
thicket-caught, death springs, ear before horn
sounding, silenced: bonsai wind shorn –
I am grafted best onto accident,
as if the wind by temple curtain was torn
as if the wilderness, death's cultured park.

9

My head, sweetmeat, fried in diplomatic hate,
presents a dainty dish – not for lips – but for eyes,
my preserved, rotted looks; a medusa – bad taste!
Canker decays sight, as death's own mirror, surprise
sets in to waste hope, unless hope is reprieved,
by the look in my gaze, searching for life,
as he changes his mind, friendship deceived,
switchblades double-edged sword for the lone tipped knife.

Putrefied fruit, pared apart; anatomy's art
will smart and start, knowledge decaying stench
that reveals and swells, amplifies smell, to outsmart
the touch of mind's eye, in the taste of the scent.
But do not deplore: dogged looks have hit the floor
I hold my head high, preserving their horror.

8

John: you rag and bone man, you one man band
of clicking locusts' lipper-honey lyres.
The lion skin stretched upon the thorn, perspires
water healed in your gnarled, believing hand.
Desert fantasy: lugging mind-fills of wet sand
grains the heat swells as it drily sires
I am a concubine to such old fires –
whetted by such god-love I am now tanned.

I rim the aching hour glass, rippling
in and out of hardening; colouring myself,
distilled in a mirage of heat's own death
that gives substance in distance fast running
across the panting belief of breath:
I too, take my deserted timer from the shelf.

lipper: leper; *lyres:* skins; *fantasy:* memory.

7

The maiden has lain with death's own blade: technology
only blundered if the lubricant soap
is unsudded to swiften blade on rope –
an unwashed maid fails death's mortality,
though must rinse out life for posterity –
otherwise execution – dying hare – must lope,
not race, with life's own vivid horoscope
pushing its features out of archeology.

I am maidenless; ride the old blunt bull
who licks the sky of triplicate suns
trodden by the virgin queen's galaxy school
spy-flogged til misinformation runs:
and yet I am equal to the reaper's tool –
like as not we both are virgins when death comes.

6

Chastelard – must death be the sound of ripping?
Black bruise in the bedclothes, silencer of shadows,
you hid in my skirts like Rizzio, held close
passion's blade – his terror; yours equipping
a small mastery of death's heart dripping
secrecy. His exposed; yours damned repose
lying in state – I above, you, in a state, rose
below when revealed, rose quick into slipping.

Heart-bludgeoned poet! Do you think I enjoy it?
Why must you force the hand of love to stiffen,
the luck of fire-salted love must be won with wit
not lost, witless. Then love's glove slips off,
the flesh-shrivelled digits, skeleton,
wherein life becomes love's death's best fit.

5

As she folds quiet into milk, I
unfold quiet into death, my blindfold
hides churning eyes that beat buttermilk gold
wet lashes trembling on the mermaid spy –
the cockleshell cuckold, chained to the eye
of this storm bound for damage by its own fair winds
a storm on its knees, listing, blind, rescinds
nothing; seeing just, the symptom of sky.

But I am god-filled with death! His sweet breath
hangs in the air of my life, my tempests
reset or resolved, like my eye-bound sight,
god lisps for death; another way to express
as my third eye sees what the gorgon insists –
my best handicap: my experienced plight.

Standing in the garden of fallen stars:
a young man is rattling my Adam rib.
So what of his wild smile, his young bull whip?
I meet the cusp on my knees, on capped hours,
as at the cliff edge, I say my prayers
balancing on the taut tightrope my crib,
crib of horse caul, crib of death, cribbed the nib
that signed me into precarious death scares:

drew me from full-blooded ink, ribbing death
who stares the knife-long edge, young maiden blade
mirror white and mirror red: mirror shade
cool disappears from hot reflection's breath –
like smoke, like mist, warm air will rise with stealth
on the stand, I'll dismay – all fade betrayed.

3

The bull-ring is hung with black flags not red,
but I have brought my own dark scarlet rag,
not gold, like my fast embroidered eye-gag,
but an underskirt for the bull, cape subtly spread
from the first blow to the last axe-sawn thread,
flagging down the vehicle of my body bag,
tricolour flag – as my woman features sag:
p'raps always was the bull; when queen is dead.

Toreador, matador, composed minotaur,
we share the same bloodlust for death's wild caper
I will take your blade in my mouth, grinning pauper
take the bull's blood jewels, polish your scraper,
death's changing shoes, rearranging slaughter –
thread-bare corridor, walls that taper.

2

I had a young head, full of sweet flowers,
delighted green lawn, cockle-shell arbour,
delicate blooms in flesh flush aurore.
young-blooded nose-gay, marigold, iris:
rose-steeped imagination of darkness,
fresh frankincense packed with myrrh and camphor
lilies gathered for the barber-jailor,
cut to stem, fade in my book of hours –

when pressed, thin prayers, between the pages:
at least preserve; at least slow desiccate
the conditions that life disengages,
slender wick of papery rusticate
rustling, arranged in death's hand enrages
life's delicate damp blossoms now aerate.

1

Oh my constricting throat, quiet, listen:
fear did not skin my muscles of old bone;
dropped into the thirsty well, my tongue – (drone
of thirstling flies, young wet for a wet sun
that bottom-up lies about being done
as each drop breaks it open); fear unspoken;
will do the coping – make blood betoken:
where tears in crystals of red water, run.

But sight has its damage, old microscope,
seen only through tense – cold lenses' tension.
The fear-plunged sun will look up, find old hope
within the well's walls, upon reflection –
well water mirror – swinging bucket on a rope –
musculature's last articulation.

II

THE BLADE

'Her lippes stirred up and down for quarter of an hour after her head was cut off.'

ROBERT WYNCKFIELD,
eyewitness at Mary Queen of Scots' execution

The scarlet timer in the wood
                    is dust itself. Flesh-shrivelled original.

Adam rib. Bribed, sagittal.

This is a hard orchard:
circus driftwood – feverish driftwood – nailed into my heart.

Flame-grinning death, resting, cools –
                    my fire-blown skeleton,
                    like new-born glass, quivers in my hot flesh –

flame-headed death is now my companion,
when we walk the glass-rattling, mirage garden,
arm-in-arm, open as an eye with torn limb, found at abandon.

He, footing damply, strike-gifted my blundered king,
stars strangled from my galaxy,
a queen mirror splashing through the room,
punctured rubies, sea bones dropped into my open tomb.

                    I hold death in my lap, suckle him,
                              perspire hot tears from every pore.
                    Who chose my eyes to send for?

Desert mastery, abortive votary,
each fire-soaked minute smokes:

Sudden wild-fire of the mirror –   John's love tears, I call you!
                              Sebastien, arrow-mouthed, I call you!

Tears survived, eyeless in exercise!
Aching, dim lengths of you!
Drown love's hair – muscles' lengths of dim eyes!

Corpses of angels: star ash gash – I call you!

Dust passion; amazed stars through violence
witch notes breaking slim,
only to language beguiled rose with love-flushed reflection,
tension, made out of delicate hiding;
death – the lovers' spiritual!

Dust passion; stars broken against the head of night –
death; witchcraft blooms starcraft,

my bled out, love flushed, young, wild skeleton!

Young troubadour!

Young troubled Bull!

Stagger into the fixed room!

O my stippled blunts of blades – the white field:

Wild, white corn scythed,
Wild, white corn lightning scryed,
Wild, white corn my concubine.

Your offering: grain studded
'tis frightened. Grave, the goddess mirror.

Kernababy, the tattered river.
Floating down with shining teeth.

Ghastly pale, the death field,
in shredded, tattered light.

Bejewelled, turned to dust: a maiden scarecrow to ward off
bad birds of my own country, a scarecrow of myself.

> Heavenly jibe: night quiver alone in the slaughter field of dreams.
> Characterised by stars: fixative of utter
> even the bones whisper galaxy in their deepest matter.

Gaunt in the corn, gaunt in the corn and whispering,
night lights the war instinct, burns the brow of the offering,
the birds that come are quixotic, dun, and mix and match the twilight.

Star-warts; foam-queen, apple-stung, rose-wreath –
tri-score roseate, sweet violet bullock,
stern and stubborn
                    stumbler into sleep.

I would suck my blood back through my face:

> a love-plashed Ophelia disintegrate,
> in wilderness, ourgilt.

The hours that stare, alternate.

> Canker of tears, sorrows, lilies, talons!
> A fine snow-blown sleep settles over us…

Floating in my designation – dust of shining flowers, flogged.

> The skull Duessa – Ophelia's float
> in my young, muddy water exfoliates
>
> god, One straight, bright iris:
> rose-steeped, rose-sealed,
> now death's new marigold –

blue-black the blood-specked roses,
        lip-flecked with love-froth thick,
           sawdust swirled in stern snowdrifts
to soak blood's toothy arrowheads – bloom's a' bloom – floating dead in
                          the belligerent weeds.

Sour luck, the starling.
               Inhabitants of dark whistle
                         before alighting, and tune again

to landing,
        tune the boards of execution.

My snail trail of delicate neck,
the slight cling of cobweb, pearled in dusk-light
the dust of eyesight, rising into vision

                the nightingale has stolen,
                the dead reeds flicker in the wind's panache,
                wrestling, unsettling, puckish moving water,
                      great cold clear air of dawn.

Dawn: violets and persimmon.

              I wake pale, in concordance with the moon;

              but the flush in my locks is crimson
                at the nape of my neck where the hair

runs red to the tip, red and shimmering,
bushel of wheat in the scarlet dawn,
              shaken down and burning.

Watermarked sword
>you ploughed the love-flushed collapse of tear.

Diction: scratch-bracelets' falling action.
I, on wrists of glass, star-littered heart,
>charm grazed.

Flame has broken, broken open onto winter
and I gaze out the fire swept land, hear the trees wildly sing as they burn.

>Once, my heart had a skeleton.

>Mermaids shall writhe in chains,
>filth covered, matted hair, madness stains.

>The sea steams in grief: girls take wild eggs to their hearts –

>>I have stripes inside my mouth like the welts of kelp,
>>the mermaid feels, passing by, rib to rib with the salt
>>tipped whip of weed, welts from keeping dumb:
>>I know how the dumb-bell feels and what causes it to numb.

>I mermaid sin – mermaids have washed in lesser bickering!

Myriads of mermaids swim in my fields;
I hold my breath, feel how the mermaid feels
in the snowy underpass of the sea – in dreams that snow with dream –
ring-gold and dip-sunk swims she, merrily,
dipped in the ink of salt-rimed pen – open,
open-armed to men.

Ringlets of stars wildening at my feet;
would you crush a star, little pipette, sweet
tear-struck rivulet, to reveal its scent

if that scent were death, and death-made were spent
ground into hours of silver-fresh sweat –

a sea ushered in black benevolence.

He has quarter violence, at full mast;
Full mast has trained the salt upwards,
to go to mouth – his water suit,
his frozen armour.

My court of falling snow:
              a plate of marigold lies
                            just beyond my severed hand.

I know the corpse's cool sun: hope.

Comet passion-suns: from astraea,
young blooded truancy,
blood-bickered, honey-lippered fear –
                            I salt-lick its fruit.

Ophelia, galaxy sun's salt: the snow suddenly among my tears, my weeping,
as made from salt – run to my heart.
Heat numbness: flowers open as silver, streaked by day
the soles of flowers run on numbness
as made mud-hot by moon rooted to the skin.
Life's lunar flavour: numbness,
wersh, the small decay moons…
the searching flowers lamp my lunar gazing under the still unwashed sun.
Then the owls pay court to demon jousting
the floorboards age without growing branches
– no spring on the carved narcissus,
the little marigold shrivels
                            and air decays the room.

My – the hot jess for death's card!

My toreador jess, the glove.
Delicate, line-caught, signature: death
                              hovers, spy-flogged

through the soundless, stoned altitude fumes.

There limbo-sight, the hand hard, his boiling venture.
                    Yet smoke, in dream for host, pacing rune and a sun:

You have my flame throne
and I crouch behind it, cowering
                              at night, when I bleed black in my sleep.

On monstrosities of dawn I rise beside the silver stream
                    and nothing can compose my shadow, save my own form
                    breaking light, whose winter husk distils soft marigold.

Fire-addled marigold, the aurore lake has spread,
gilt is on your petal and your petal sun-slaked pearl:

                              shinbone of lion,
                              adamantine: milk sop of virgin.
A dawn-lake of scales glitters
tear-dark, changes, flush-flamed to stars.

                    god's sawdusted water, death airs
sung.

Faint that moth, ever close as of flame my barque
                              shudder-shone

on the waters: light the death air
the sound of sweet, of sweet floating queens
like lighthouse driftwood into birds,

the driftwood you fear: killings, dark and clear,
dark, darkening...
dreamed water of the world's faint, smouldering killings:
                              carries dream's flame figurehead.
Milk sings, rising,
              cut from darkness,
                          from my lactating face of dreams.

                          Reindeer milk and aniseed,
                          washing polyps in the dark
                          crying young crustaceans
                          breed, listless, into hare...

Tomb risen in milk-fields of steam;
unguent of soured stars glistening.
                    ponds of milk, pools of milk, the reindeer's tears
                    from teats of eyes, murky whirlpools.

   Let us not escape into milk-white woods
        of the roses that burn in the deadly carpet of the mind's womb –
        dare not, smell the death vapour of the burning rose –
snuffed by waters of heaven –

Milk euphoric, a platitude of resonant stars,
my mystery, milkhood, rises off the lunar fields,
rising star-dusk, dark, lactating whorls,
sapped in the sorrow-lanes that run down the night
tapped from stellar-thicket grass,
sap of reluctant hares...

The corpse-copse rippling – yet smoke, in dream.
I: made like wooed, fell to my knees.

The stage, like time: sap beneath reaped bark.
Wood: pressing rings' scarlet death-hood.

Flame's to flame, estranged.
Dream, caught in cups, courts sleep – the only audience night-visions keep –
I must be drowsy-smashed, limped on life,
to hold the stare of death's keen knife.

Look you, the mirror's bare. I logged the ring of wood,
snapped the thickening, thickening twig, spilt the gum
that evidenced, dream-surges pulsing from the tree.

Death: apparition's innermost hope –
fire-traiked ice upon mirage: death:
                              I pursue curse.

On in cold nutrition, I constellation,
                    stormy with my own silence: verity.

                    My ever-wild linnet, rose below into ghost –
                    apparition: death's innermost hope.

Young edge: a garden, who full-blooded from smoke
and wild dismay – prays, balancing on the
cribbed sheet of mirror – on knife-long knees.

So cooled, death shade,
                    lone territory of bone stitched hours.

Understand how water's fast failing stars
                    but in constellation, water's falling boy labours
            climbing wild, close, trace to trace.

Snow-splashed memory,
he leans at the bank,
hanging young down to water.
                              Quick potassium hovers,
                              life his manhood wood.

Art: will of Adam,
frankincense bone, lifted, yields.

Me, iris white, the capped blade,
the cusp-wild blade in the garden
meets the bewilderment stare of the young man
all if rose coloured flesh is gun,
my smoking prayers balancing
on the edge of thought like the balancing rib.

Kiss my labours, ever-wild! In pan dark we move,
smokeless to pipes.

Splintered linnet; tuneless young tune,
love's desecration.

Kiss the storm within the wood!
Kiss the storm, misunderstood!

The war-cry, eye,
water-music of demise –
moon-plush, his plashless cloak.
He swamps the water-eye of the earth,
that she might stamp it out.

Spread, she walks as night air
and he kneels upon her pearlescent teeth,
polished policer of lunar grief.

Breath pen; conjured star clouds encode –
lips' arrow; love's ribs course the fingertips to heart,
conjured of ploughs, encode –
love's shallow!

Quickening the hand, cross-hatching the self –
inconsiderate breath!

Conjured, the arrow's delicate fingertip!
The inconsiderate night pen of blood spilled lip!
                              The stellar stealth of maidenhead.

Grim ribs to sand blade –
all I ask is that the blood's spilled below love's pen
hand hatching, ask sweat – the wet pen – the aim of the code:

the flashing arrow's reverse plough,
damp systems, bend and pull.

Sand stars who delicate, quickening lips encode –
sand-hatching sagittal blade:
                              desk equipment of the heart.

It is said of the flame-possessed, the gold must
now choose men, as muse myself,
could take her hand, her jewels, her mouth,
weeping with that starry love,

                France, I lift your gentle mouth to my like-minded mouth,

France, gold-danced within
like rubies, the brooding self,

                              would sometimes rub against window
                              panes, genie one, pensive pearls and birds
                              held in a flame of snow,
                              fettered in flame-like weeping.

Hair with brooding breath,
little nipped jewels, a clutch, little wild-fire
pattering onto the floor.

France – I stub your
toes on rings, and Scotland one through
the nose, and my queen, a shining disc
of polished oak,

                    a throwing quoit
                    to cross-slice your constricted throat.

Storm-signature of birds in an inkwell,
                  feather restless, sermon emerging,
                  such spluttered feverish flex,
                  a goddess working over quills:

The explode still hawked, Bess,
meteor fine from fingers' dream,
fingers scribed in jess for lemon – a ghost-comet's skin flex.

It is not death's skull that comes peering
but my own that skins his of bone
in the clearing.

Touch: diplomatic knowledge,
       anatomy's dainty canker,

                  he looks up to my horror

my head as friendship, suddenly
my double edge gaze,
                  preserving bad looks, swells.

This year is shriven in hawk gauntlets,
martyr: mine beat of wounds, juddering, falls,
fearing limbs, as pulse stars flogged,
charred, death-shafts of ransom darkening.

The arena mirror breath, dream-healed,
in delicate attempt he glows, like your greater hate –
love's mind; the dead betrayed.

His end limbs, death lies beat,
twitching stars in his meat,
price: charred, end staggers, as of drowned,
dawn heads of the arrow... the sewer stoned.

Mine their god beheaded:
darkening universe of birth wounds,
whispers close, blubbering and patterned –
slowly beaten –

> 'I use trophies and won its limbs,
> bones my holster whispers,
> holstered through flame,
> bones darkening his trophies...'

Fallen salt, ever-wild;

> cold bone through rock-face like my race
> cold dreams in weathered snow.

Rock-face of cold high seasoned tears it heats,
it falls on the dreams' nakedness: my end salt though hunted melts,
tears saline, dual, blow my cover
ever-wild dreams with snow as heat;
fallen cold's extremes.

> Lick stag fear, thirst sung!
> Lick mineral christ from my potassium womb!

I lie down to the bone, from deer that the children wore
now, my headless lick, Christ death's gown,
stag transubstantiation.
A salt-lick hide, tongue grappled crown.
The children snowing from licking, lapping up legend bone.

Thirst marrow – nutrition – comb, tomb, the saline room:

                                  Locked in, I drown.

A red wind and a skinned lion cub
he sweats in bleeds; a maritime disease,

                            le lion rouge, mon coeur
                            near the river,

The stream spreads its skin
and lifts it, glistening.

Come red, by lightening on the salt wet beach,
whose knees are sand, who fell, like the corrupted towers
of beached castles.

Rusted marigold: the canary-mated dark,
flesh full lilies, young-blooded blossoms
imagination enrages thin, green pressed and
the snood of night-ness nods
flesh wick, the marigold, fresh the barber-jailor
from his mould, at the command of a thick cockle shell.

Delicate myrrh, full pressed,
papery dawn – in camphor green – stenches prayers:
rose-steeped marigold; death's a blossom's head,
the book of death's least preserve:
frankincense nose-gay, fresh to the end page,

                                now delighted, fades.

This island of backward horizon:

                      horizon-shy the opening
                      pawning hard, blood-bickered heaven
                      the black, blood-bickered island,
                      its heaven pressed deep,
                      saddling, I seasoned within swallow
                      chewed on rebellion, the old wizened,
                      bejewelled dream queene.

Prison – is that star-littered mirror intensity?

So diction, scratch has destiny?

Moon-shaven night; star-pocked chin: stubble of abrasion.
Bars, diamond: necklace minions, punctured when imprisoned,
in the nightjar wood, shining stars of the lesson,
trembling marks in the sparkling hour glass;
diamond marks' compression.

Open stars! Star-shackled destiny!
The mirror: a heart-torn safe –
do quick, what the glass sights now –
Soundless death, my diamond smart.
Diamond tear-sounded death –

haunt the stony hour.
Shaved: grave and moon-burnt.

Bombaze-smack:

so bombaze tears open!

Rapid crustacean's histories,
encrusted jewels in the eyes of the gods.

Star flower hurts – embedded in jewel flower – hurts.

Tints of star luminettes.

I, ever jewels,
your sewer burns seal.

My were-mineral: diamond.

So sheer, the star:
Death's dream-ear:

Grave lode magician
couples the reflection

dead slender camphor of gaze,
myrrh thin pen,
reflection of hard well's sparkling trace,
water horizon.

My poor ambulance, limping to the block
greeted in tears, taking cockle stock,
no spring on the carved narcissus
and the little marigold shrivels –

A cold wind that cups the desert's collops,
a fire-white hood of grief
foal-caul of white-hot ember
crushed to glittering diamond tears
bleaching out the blood from slaughter
but waking with the brilliant flash –
the killer firework glitter –
swiftly aged to gleam.

                  Torture splits the young orchard.
                  Will you fill your cheeks with guilt?
                  Pock-marked the stars on the guttural shelf.
                  She squeezes disease out of health.

Stuffed into my graffiti bag:

Mary's skull; cotton picked over will,
pocked of will: diamond over gold.

Circus rebel tapestry... Eden's
here in sins.
I graffiti paw, in scope or the thread
all silk, all hare's hope.

I magician coupled sins,
scale Eve's.

Boredom's tapestry: here beast, lope, here frayed.

Here, wildest taboo, wildest flies a votary,
needled in flicking beast,
woodland's skins furred:
bestial votary
boredom's ark.

                  Sew twisted from the animal scurry.

Rope-dense, the axe-man's wick,
spluttered life's gnarled, interlinked flakes:
young death's mist-suckled face
dead composed stars – a visible downpour –

Putrefied on arrow, he cures his hot lesson –

                      The sewer's a steam-bath!

I felt fear rippling, muscled in the wind.
                 Dark flags strangle, collapse.

Standing on earth, my lord,
from first colouring's song, my mark's smack.
Horse caul... foal caul; his hope's throat throttling.

Tree of gristle, swung.
Tree of singing virgin heads
white night at Christmas,
auburn lawn,
spinning on warm tongues.

The plumb-line.
My hung-spun apples, rotating blackly on the branches.
Distorted, the eyes return.

The archer quivers; hard-stare; nutritious.

Sin stallion, little jet
skinned, like the sun,
in brilliance molten, the moon bewails.

Her diamante arrows slim,
like long white fingers plucking the sibilant heart from him
her nectar worn in the low sloping woods at dawn,
in rivers of white gold that fiercely burn
within the sight-lines of the rising sun,

Watch her nithing horse, descend, drown, re-emerge,
ploughing gold in the burn as it turns,
and her wet feet, dragged the hem,
drags the leaves my burnished throne – a horse chair, thrown –

Heart-salted, dirty water, scrying bones of stallion
dried in the dawn, hope's throat throttling,
the dim-eyed nag, blue-glazed eye and stringy mane,
been whetted in the butcher shop, foamed with gristle
on the floor:

bullion of animal dream,
bullion of scareling calf
bullion of copped harm's dull

                                    thud on the wooden arm.

Dreams' confidence schools
silver walled water wells.

So hard sawdust explodes,
mistress wound, stern intern.

Shadow pleading, begging, sobbing, panting
dragged along by stun-ambled shambling –
cursing and licking at ankles swollen –

this delicate burr, this hook-caught death.

Turn, dirty river, turn!

The pauper bucket, splashing, fills.

Eviction! The mirror cooled.
Animal open: apparition's figurehead.

The salt-water expression
stills.

CODA

Mary Stuart lived her life as a great poet and like all poets of political assassination, created a death of sheer poetry. Imprisoned for nearly twenty years, this belle rebelle was the star of the European courts and experienced every major crisis a woman can encounter: rape, miscarriage, illness, murder, attempted suicide, bereavement of parents at a young age and eventually execution. She had three husbands, an estranged son, an entangled court and adversaries in the form of the magic practising Elizabethan secret service. Mary was the student of one of France's greatest poets Pierre de Ronsard who – with his Pleiades – valued the young royal hugely. She was their astraea, their bright star. Through Ronsard, Mary Stuart takes her place in French literature alongside Verlaine and Rimbaud. She is the absolute of French noir, the belle *and* the bête; the bête noire. She is also the manifest spirit of troubadour which later spawned chanson. She is the femme of the gallant code of medieval French chivalry – the muse and the performer; sister to Joan of Arc.

The first part of this book, 'The Descent', comprises thirty-five sonnets, one for each step Mary Queen of Scots descended in the great oak staircase said to have been taken from Fotheringhay castle. The mostly Petrarchan sonnets draw their imagery from her life's history, her own writing and the writing of those around her, including the great Pierre de Ronsard and are written as if in her own voice. Part two, 'The Blade' comprises a sequence of the thirty-five sonnets in part one chewed or chawed up, extending the cut-up technique of Brion Gysin and William Burroughs. The chaw ups are literal: spat, ground, muttered and gnashed for the fifteen minutes the lips in Mary's decapitated head were said to move. After chewing up the sonnet manuscript, I reconstructed the second sequence from the tattered, masticated pellets, laying them out to dry and allowed them to determine and suggest the form and imagery of 'The Blade'. Equally, this section is designed to take approximately fifteen minutes to be read or to read.

Much has been written on Mary Queen of Scots and she has inspired a plethora of poetic responses. I am indebted to William Byrd to William Wordsworth, from Robert Burns to Lord Darnley. This work sprang, however, not from a compulsion to respond to Mary poetically as a historically inspiring figure but to exorcise a recurring dream set in St Giles Cathedral, Edinburgh, in which I seem to approach the event of her execution among terrifying tombs and up a large oak staircase. In the dream I navigate towards the death chamber, mounting the long flight of heavy wooden stairs, but of course never reach the top.

MacGillivray,

Edinburgh

NOTES

SONNET 35

Mary Queen of Scots was born on December 7th or 8th 1542 at Linlithgow Palace. Her birth date formally aligns her with the tropical astrological attributes of the archer, under Sagittarius, and the first lines argue with the bow, that it is not used to direct the arrow straight into her heart; i.e. that her own nature does not shoot itself.

The name Mary derives from the Icelandic word 'maer' meaning virgin or maid.

Maidenhead: a term for the hymen.

'maidenhead's face': a play on the 'maiden'; the Scottish guillotine, in reference to Mary's love of word games and puns which she made frequent use of in her own poetry. The maiden was said to have been brought to Scotland by the Earl of Morton who was impressed by its efficiency but who died himself under its blade in 1581, for his part in the murder of Mary's husband, Darnley. Mary, of course, was beheaded by axe but the maiden here presents a more formidable force in delivering an accurate and swift death and is used as short-hand for all decapitations as well as in relation to motifs of femininity, purity, virginity and maidenhood evoked by sup-porters of Mary and catholicism and of Elizabeth and her staunch single status as 'the virgin queen', on the other.

'which, before the blade, love's death made sallow' refers to her sudden pallor after the death of her first husband, the dauphin Francois; long before she faced the execution block. This change in her complexion is noted by her tutor and mentor, Pierre De Ronsard: 'your fair throat wears no finery but its pallor for a jewel...' and by Mary herself: 'Deep in my eyes and heart / A portrait has its place / Which shows the world my hurt / In the pallor of my face / Pale as when violets fade/ True love's becoming shade.' ('Ode on the Death of Her Husband, King Francis II, When He Was Sixteen and She Was Seventeen Years Old', 1560, tr. Robin Bell)

'Or reverse your course to shift the stellar sand'; as if her own star sign constructed the execution apparatus of her death – i.e. suggestive of her own constellar pre-destination and nature, the star dust of which she herself was made.

SONNET 34

'On Sunday 29th January, between midnight and one o'clock in the morning, the heavens gave their own portent that the end was not far off, for a great flame of fire illuminated the windows of the queen's room three times. The light was bright enough to read by, and blinded the guards stationed beneath her chamber... This supernatural warning, if warning it was, was certainly borne out by events... a more rational explanation might be that the mysterious fire was produced by a comet. In Elizabethan England, comets were traditionally associated with the deaths of famous people, or as Shakespeare put it in *Julius Caesar*: "When beggars die, there are no comets seen; the heavens themselves blaze forth the deaths of princes." ' – Antonia Fraser.

'This sheaf of papers, comet ridden, is restless': The trifold comet display heralded Elizabeth's signature on Mary's death warrant three days later which had been carefully placed in the midst of a sheath of papers by William Davison, her secretary. Comets were commonly misinterpreted as meteors at the time.

'a three-score phoenix god scribed your amen': the image of the phoenix also refers to Mary's mother's impresa (symbol) of the phoenix. Marie de Guise's accompanying motto of this mythical bird rising from the flames was 'En Ma Fin Git Ma Commencement': 'In My End Lies My Beginning'. The image in the sonnet collapses Elizabeth with Mary's mother, suggesting kinship but also the resurrection of one motif at the expense of another; Elizabeth will always be overshadowed by Mary and, necessarily, so too will Mary by Elizabeth.

SONNET 31

Is addressed to Elizabeth I.

SONNET 30

'I made an impression; my ring on wood': the staircase at the Talbot Inn, Oundle, is said to be the one from Fotheringhay castle before the building was demolished by order of James VI; its masonry distributed throughout the British Isles. Legend has it that the small impression of a ring on one of the landing newels was made by Mary on her descent down the staircase to her execution on the morning of February 8th, 1587. The clear indent of a crown on the ring is still there, marked on the wood. This sonnet also serves as counterpoint to Ronsard's striking description of Mary's infamous white hands (which once disrupted an escape attempt from Lochleven Island, when the boatman – unable to see her face, recognised her by a long, slim and white hand and returned her to the castle). 'Your lovely hands boast no ornament save their natural whiteness, your slender fingers, like saplings of unequal growth, bear no precious rings…'

SONNET 29

In addition to being a skilled sportswoman, huntress and rider, Mary Stuart was accomplished in needlework which became essential to fill the monotonous hours of imprisonment she was subjected to in the last years of her life. The poem positions her within a rebel tapestry comprised of strange beasts. As a child brought up with tropical birds and other creatures in the French court, Mary developed a palpable love of animals – evident at the end in the account of the small Highland terrier that crept from her skirts after her execution, sat at her neck and subsequently died despite being carried off and washed of Mary's blood. Many of Mary's embroideries have simple symbolic messages – the cat and mouse, for example – seen to depict the cruel political game played by Elizabeth in her entrapment of her cousin queen. Other small coded images can be deciphered but the suggestion in this poem is that Mary, whose coded letters were seized and easily translated by English spies associated with the Star Chamber, resorted to needlework rebelry worked at in stitched and threaded motifs which included one of her own personal symbols; the marigold open to the sun. As

Margaret Swain describes: 'the "devising of works" served not only to occupy her fingers and to fill the long empty days, but the design could have a double meaning, or an emblem with a tart motto, which would exercise her wit and help assuage her burning sense of injustice'. The poetry and needlework of Mary Queen of Scots both present a stitched and scribed landscape of ciphers, emblems and covert, punned messages. Because her written work – in letters, coded messages and poems was so carefully monitored during captivity, Mary may well have focussed her deliberations and attention on particular motifs to meditate on her next move but also to communicate outwardly something of her frustration.

SONNET 28

There are conflicting accounts regarding Mary overhearing the construction of her execution scaffold during the three days before her execution. Given the announcement on the eve of her death late in the evening this seems unlikely but when the reader is confronted with a description of the black lagging and the stage within the Great Hall at Fotheringhay, there must have been a certain amount of formal preparation. This sonnet takes thematic inspiration from Robert Burns' 'Tam O' Shanter': 'Five tomahawks, wi' blude red-rusted / Five scimitars, wi' murder crusted / A garter which a babe had strangled / A knife, a father's throat had mangled' in combination with the description of the large axe used to execute the queen; 'like those with which they cut wood', observed Bourgoing, eyewitness of the execution.

> 'Steel in her swordhand, poison in her left,
> Let death rant on, an old age scythe
> All down at harvest...
> though apocalypse fuse earth and stars'
>
> GEORGE BUCHANAN

SONNET 27

Associated with formal magic in relation to Elizabeth's secret service, Dr John Dee is informed by his assistant, Edward Kelley in 1583 that he has marked in his diary a dream in which the hand of a beautiful woman is cut off by a tall black man. In a subsequent séance, Dee then perceives this to be a vision of Mary Queen of Scots and so becomes aware of her pending death. Speculation positions Walsingham as the tall, black man – the man whom Elizabeth called her moor and who referred to himself as Ethiopian. A small historical detail from Mary's execution scene describes how she knelt to the block positioning a small hand on either side of her face. The executioner's assistant moved her arms so that her hands would not be cut off.

'The story appears to be straightforward according both to Dee's angels and traditional legend: Samael/Choronzon tempted Eve, and was banished into the world with them, and Watchers were set over the creation to maintain its bounds. However, traditional legend holds a surprise.' – Colin Low, *Liber Logaeth*

'Samael and his angels were banished to a dark dungeon, where they still languish, their faces haggard, their lips sealed; and are now known as the Watchers.' – John Dee, as quoted from Robert Graves & Raphael Patai, *Hebrew Myths: The Book of Genesis*

'This legend is recounted in a book that Dee could not have read because it was lost in Europe until it was brought back from Ethiopia by the Scots adventurer James Bruce of Kinnaird in 1773. By an astonishing coincidence this happens to be yet another Book of Enoch. Although it has been dubbed one of the most boring books ever written, anyone with an interest in Dee and Kelly's conversations with angels should read it. Too much attention has been devoted to the magical system communicated by the angels to Dee; this occupies a relatively small part of the several hundred pages in Dee's transcripts. The angels have a great deal to say. It is interesting to meet again many of Dee's angels in the visions recounted in the Ethiopian Book of Enoch.' – Robert Graves & Raphael Patai, *Hebrew Myths: The Book of Genesis*.

SONNET 26

'A man weighed before war, returns from war dead-weight': Greek Kouros were said originally to have been

144

recreated to the exact weight, height and likeness of significant men lost at war or at sea to reproduce them as statues for long-term posterity.

SONNET 25

'Bricked Sebastien licks his wounds, sewer bound': sonnet 25 investigates Mary's imagined sympathy for other martyrs; in this case Sebastien who was the only saint to be martyred 'twice', by being shot at with arrows but ultimately bricked to death in Roman sewers. The line 'by death, my bones are used as trophies' comes from the controversial casket letters: 'though death may use my bones as trophies', which are variously attributed in whole or in part to Mary by her detractors and dismissed as fictitious inventions by her defenders.

SONNET 24

'Or if you sometimes have wished'. Constructed as a fictitious sonnet to Ronsard from Mary. The rapidly ageing, imprisoned Queen tried to honour her beloved tutor with a poem to thank him for the 1583 book of verse he dedicated to her in addition to a sonnet he sent to her in captivity, but felt she had failed, as Robin Bell notes: 'Mary found it impossible to write a good poem in reply... After the second line in the second verse, she wrote and scored out "Or if you sometimes have wished".'

SONNET 21

The sun and marigold was one of Mary's personal motifs accompanied by the Latin motto 'Non Inferiora Secutus', meaning 'Not following lower things'. Margaret Swain notes 'the symbol or impresa of Marguerite of Navarre, it was taken by Mary as her own with the motto "Sa Virtu m'Atire" ('Its strength draws me'), an anagram of her name MARIE STVART.'

The repetition of red in the sonnet denotes Mary's infamous auburn hair but is also traditionally associated with magic and the fiery archer sign of Sagittarius.

SONNET 20

In angel's weed I saw a noble queen
Above the skies in sphere of crystal light.
Who on earth bit long before was seen
Of divers heinous crimes to be indict.
By false suspect and jealousy of those
Whom fear had wrought to be her mortal foes.

WILLIAM BYRD, Angel's Weed,

SONNET 18

James Hepburn, 4th Earl of Bothwell is a controversial character. Presumed to have taken Mary by force in order to secure a marriage, he comes across as brutish, powerful, enigmatic and passionate. All husbands involved with Mary met untimely deaths but Bothwell's fate was perhaps the worst – and certainly worse then Mary's. Captured by the Danish following his escape north from Carberry Hill on June 15th, 1567 to land on the Norwegian coast, for a previous crime against a previous fiancée, Anna Thronsden and various unpaid Scandinavian debts. Thrown into a succession of Danish prisons he died insane in Dragsholm Castle having been chained to a pillar in a cell half his height, covered in his own matted hair and filth. His mummified remains are still displayed to the curious traveller at the small church in Fårevejle. A curious aside to the subject of Bothwell is that the only known poem by Rizzio, 'The Ballad of Love', written in 1564, contains the lines 'Love is made a god by those who feed his fires / some die for him, others he keeps in shackled locks and chains', which could have been written with Bothwell in mind. The image of the post or pole is echoed in the naming of a stalactite by Mary Queen of Scots in Poole's Cavern near Buxton, which she visited in 1582.

SONNET 17

Diamonds are frequently associated with Mary. Her wedding dress for her first marriage to Francis was 'shimmering white and ablaze with diamonds'. 'Adamis Loquitir', 'The

146

Diamond Speaks' written in 1562, exists in translation only, the original now lost, and was sent to Elizabeth by Mary along with a ring set with a diamond. While Mary playfully and expertly positions and re-positions the voice of the diamond, sonnet 17 – in addition to sonnets 22 and 20 – treats the notion of compression, from which anything carbon can exact a diamond, as Mary's own compression or claustrophobia. In this sonnet, the diamond referred to is created from Mary's dried and compressed blood.

'ensanguined block' – Wordsworth.

SONNET 16

Poem to Rizzio (or Riccio).

This piece by Rizzio; sung at a great feast in Holyrood House in the winter of 1564 provides an interesting premonition of both Rizzio and Bothwell's fates:

> 'What is the power that the world calls love?
> … is made a god, by those who feed his fires,
> some die for him, others he keeps in
> shackled locks and chains.'

SONNET 15

Mary's heart remains buried anonymously at the site of Fotheringhay. This poem refers to her haar clad landing at Leith on August 19th, 1561, an arrival which was seen as an ill omen; particularly by John Knox who thought her arrival one of 'sorrow, dolour, darkness and impiety' for Scotland. He proved to be one of her greatest adversaries.

As Mary was waiting for her ship to depart for Scotland in 1561, a fishing boat sank before her eyes with all its crew. She exclaimed: 'What a sad augury for a journey!' As the ship sailed away she kept her eyes on the French coast until it was totally out of sight repeating over and over: 'Adieu France, adieu donc ma chère France… je pense ne vous revoir jamais plus' (Farewell dear France, I believe never to see you again). Mary's sorrow was justified; she never did return to France, neither alive nor dead.

SONNET 14

This poem refers to the reins that Mary was said to have embroidered for her estranged young son who was taken from her when he was one year old, now at Arundel Castle, Sussex. The pun on rein and reign is in alignment with Mary's use and love of punning and the image of the thistle relates to the breastplate of the reins which comprised rose, pink, pomegranate and thistle.

The caul is a fine membrane which sometimes covers the faces of newborn babies. Mary's son James VI was born with the lucky caul (a piece of amniotic sac) which, according to the superstition, guaranteed that he would not meet his death by drowning.

SONNET 13

'I see that it is snowing in my tomb' was written in connection to a recurring dream about Mary Queen of Scots' execution, set in St Giles Cathedral, Edinburgh among ominous tombs. The later discovery of Ronsard's poem 'On the Death of Mary' had curious resonance: 'Sleeping at dark of night, I seem to see / Half-open, in my dream a tomb appear / Within it Death was lying, pale with fear/ Beneath I read: Le Tombeau de Marie.' (Tr. Charles Graves)

SONNET 12

See the note for sonnet 35.

SONNET 11

References to Duessa and the 'non-fairie queene' draw on Edmund Spenser's famous work *The Faerie Queene* whose 1596 edition allegorically recreates Mary Stuart's impromptu trial. In Book 5, Canto IX, stanzas 36-50, we find the tragic queen personified as 'Duessa' and her queenly counterpart Elizabeth, as the noble 'Mercilla' (note the suggestion of mercy which was ironically lacking from Elizabeth towards Mary throughout the trial and execution). Elizabeth's apparent reticence to commit regicide is curiously depicted through the inclusion of a three-stanza break at the conclusion of Canto IX [5]. As a literary event, Mary's execution occurs at the start of Canto X.

Astraea is what the French poetry circle, the Pleiades, called Mary as their bright star and also referred to her as the dawn, the aurore. Brantome: 'In her fifteenth year her beauty began to radiate from her like the sun in a noonday sky.' Ronsard: 'O belle et plus que belle et agréable Aurore.' Joachim du Bellay: 'Nature et art ont en votre beauté, / Mis tout le beau dont la beauté s'assemble.'

SONNET 9

According to eye witness accounts of her execution, Mary's head, when held aloft, fell from the auburn lawn or wig she wore, causing consternation and dismay among eyewitnesses who remarked on the sudden and dramatic difference between the living and speaking queen and her now lifeless severed head with its aged expression. Here the medusa is called upon and Mary is an image of horror, necessarily shocking in her theatrical manipulation of her own execution as religious martyrdom which displayed courage and flair.

'dogged looks': 'Then one of the executioners, pulling off her garters, espied her little dog which was crept under her clothes, which could not be gotten forth but by force, yet afterward would not depart from the dead corpse, but came and lay between her head and her shoulders, which being imbrued with her blood was carried away and washed, as all things else were that had any blood was either burned or washed clean, and the executioners sent away with money for their fees, not having any one thing that belonged unto her. And so, every man being commanded out of the hall, except the sheriff and his men, she was carried by them up into a great chamber lying ready for the surgeons to embalm her.' (Robert Wynkfielde)

SONNET 8

Mary petitions John as a like-minded, beheaded martyr, using word play on desert and deserted.

SONNET 7

Further allusions to the Scottish Maiden, whose rope had to be frequently soaped so that the mechanism ran smoothly and caused minimal distress to the victim. Here the play on maiden as a female virgin, punitive machine within the traditional theme of 'Death and the Maiden' is connected to both Elizabeth and Mary as virgins in relation to death.

'Spy-flogged' is a phrase used to highlight the political relentlessness in terms of the early English Secret Service through the 007 John Dee and Walsingham in framing Mary.

SONNET 6

Pierre de Bocosel de Chastelard or Chatelard was a twenty-two year old French poet (also schooled by Ronsard, whom he quoted at his execution) who developed a dangerous obsession with Mary Queen of Scots and after his second offence was put to death by beheading in 1562 at St Andrews. This sonnet alludes to Mary's severity in endorsing such heavy punishment to a young gallant; a French court poet and one with whom she had conversed with frequently. He was found twice in her bedchamber, hiding beneath the bed and was firstly thrown out and subsequently warned not to return to court, and secondly, when he had the foolhardy audacity to follow the Queen to St Andrews, was tried and executed but not before Mary – discovering Chastelard herself – cried out for him to be put to death there and then. 'Adieu, the most beautiful and most cruel princess of the world' were his last words. Perhaps he was a Huguenot spy, and certainly there were rumours, sent to dishonour Mary's reputation. Rizzio, too, was suspected of being a Papal messenger or spy but working for Mary, rather than against. The sound of ripping in the sonnet refers to Rizzio's fingers clutching Mary's skirts as he was dragged off and stabbed over fifty times, having first been wounded while still cowering behind her in the royal apartments at Holyrood Palace.

SONNET 5

'As she folds quiet into milk' is inspired by Mary's embroidery of a maid milking a reindeer in which the figure of the girl seems blindfold and so an uncanny pre-configuration of her own blindfold on her execution day. Mary derived many animal emblems from Conrad Gesner's 1560 *Icones Animalum* whose lavish and detailed woodcuts of wild mammals, birds and fishes provided the animal-loving Queen with rich inspiration.

The image of the mermaid is derogatory and is taken from the famous cartoon posted up in Edinburgh of the hare (Bothwell's family crest) and mermaid (Mary – the mermaid as synonymous with prostitute) after Darnley's suspicious and violent murder. The placard clearly associated Mary with the crime in the public eye. Nonetheless, the skull of Darnley (Mary's second husband) is now in the Royal College of Surgeons in London and bears the telltale pitted marks of Syphilis. Darnley's notorious promiscuity would have finally had the better of him had he not in fact died a little earlier during the Kirk o' Field incident.

Adultery first became a capital offence in the reign of Mary Queen of Scots although its introduction was more to do with her High Kirk Minister, John Knox, than herself. For this was the time of the Protestant Reformation. The laws against adulterers were extended by her son James VI.

The cockleshell is used in association with a nursery rhyme that may relate to Mary I or Mary Queen of Scots; 'Mary, Mary, quite contrary, how does your garden grow? With silver bells and cockle shells and pretty maids all in a row.' The cockle is also a common weed that often invades the tilled fields and grows among with the planted grain. It symbolises wickedness invading the good field of the Church. 'Let thistles grow up to me instead of wheat, and thorns instead of barley' [Job 31:40]. Purple thistles still grow on the site of Mary's execution and are nicknamed Queen Mary's tears. Ronsard: 'That living and dead, your body be but roses... A thistle's, to me, a bonny rose.'

SONNET 3

This sonnet plays on the word 'bull' in relation to a Papal

Bull issued in 1570 'excommunicating Elizabeth and releasing her Catholic subjects from their loyalty to her' and the surname of Mary's executioner; Bull, thereby recreating her as both bull and toreador with her dark scarlet petticoat worn to die as a Catholic martyr. The poem was inspired by Lorca's 'Lament for the Death of a Bullfighter' in mind, situating both Lorca and Mary Stuart as poets who suffered political assassination.

SONNET 2

'I had a young head, full of sweet flowers' keeps in mind Robert Burns' 'Lament of Mary, Queen of Scots on the Approach of Spring' – perhaps the greatest poem written to her. Burns would have been familiar with Ronsard's lines: 'Lost in your thoughts and bathing with the crystal droplets of your tears, you walked sorrowfully down the long avenues of the great gardens of... Fontainebleau... the whole gardens were filled with the whiteness of your veils like the sails which billow from the mast over the ocean wave... the white-clad swans...'

'barber-jailor' is a play on 'barber surgeon', used to suggest the roughness of Mary's executioner and the implement used to sever her head.

DECONSTRUCTED SONNETS

'kernababy': 'the last gleanings of the last field are bound up in a rude imitation of the human shape and dressed in some rag-tags of finery. The image has fallen into conservative hands of children, but of old "the maiden" was a regular image of the harvest goddess' – in relation to astraea and virgo." Quotation taken from the myth of the Maiden of the Wheat Field, by Andrew Lang in *Custom and Myth*, to add an additional layer of meaning to both the maiden and astraea in the context of Mary's death ravaged form post execution.

'mermaids': Keats: 'the mermaid of the zodiac' from 'Lines

On the Mermaid Tavern' situates Mary more closely within the derogatory image of the mermaid and hare – as a commoner and prostitute like those found in inns such as the Mermaid Tavern but also subject to her zodiacal destiny as evident in Sonnet 35.

'wersh': tasteless, lacking flavour, weak or insipid.

'moon-plush, his plashless cloak': influenced by the anonymous 1588 portrait of Sir Walter Raleigh in the National Portrait Gallery of which 'research and conservation has revealed a patch of wavy water beneath the crescent moon. Symbolic of Elizabeth I as the moon goddess Cynthia, the motif is also found in Raleigh's poetry, and indicates his willingness to be controlled by the queen as the moon controls the tides'. Raleigh presents good counterpoint to Mary's solar marigold sign and Elizabeth's preference for pearlescent purity.

'poor ambulance': 1798, 'mobile or field hospital', from French *(hôpital) ambulant*, literally 'walking (hospital)', from Latin *ambulantem* (nominative *ambulans*), present participle of *ambulare* 'to walk' (see *amble*).

A nithing pole consisted of a long, wooden pole with a recently cut horse head at the end (Scandinavian imagery).

'stern': Scots for star – a pun on the English 'stern'.

ACKNOWLEDGEMENTS

My many thanks to the staff at: Westminster Abbey; St Giles Cathedral; the Talbot Inn, Oundle; Holyrood Palace; Edinburgh Castle and the Special Collections at the National Library of Scotland for allowing access to the last letter of Mary Queen of Scots. Thanks also to Aly Barr and Kaite Welsh at Creative Scotland. Thank you to Nancy Campbell, Damian Le Bas, Francis McGreechin and Niall McDevitt for their spirit and friendship. I am indebted to the wisdom, understanding and support of Neil Astley. My deepest gratitude to Cairine MacGillivray for our many excursions into the hinterland across the years to visit hanging trees, abbeys and bells heard ringing in forests.

Sonnets 4 and 21 with their equivalent destroyed counterparts from *In My End Is My Beginning* were published in *Test Centre Seven*, December 2016.

'AILM – PINE' from *The Gaelic Garden of the Dead* was published online in *MONK*, November 2018.

'IOGH – YEW' and 'Testimony of the Rocks' from *The Gaelic Garden of the Dead* is published in the *New River Press Yearbook 2018-19*.

MACGILLIVRAY

Kirsten Norrie writes poetry under her matrilineal name, MacGillivray. Educated at Oxford University, she is the author of three poetry collections (Red Hen, USA, 2013), *The Nine of Diamonds: Surroial Mordantless* (Bloodaxe Books, 2016) and *The Gaelic Garden of the Dead* (Bloodaxe Books, 2019). She is a tutor at the Poetry School, London, and in 2018 founded The Oxford School of Poetry. Norrie has worked in translation, collaborating with Latvian poets in Riga for Latvian Literature, was one of three featured Scottish poets for the Queensland Poetry Festival 2015 and has received numerous Creative Scotland awards for her writing which has appeared in publications such as *Test Centre*, *Magma*, *The Scotsman*, New River Press, *The Poetry Review* and *Modern Poetry in Translation,* and on BBC Radio 3's *Late Junction* and *The Verb*.